Randomized Controlled Trials

Questions, Answers, and Musings

Second edition

Alejandro R Jadad MD, DPhil, FRCPC
Chief Innovator and Founder, Centre for Global eHealth
Innovation
Canada Research Chair in eHealth Innovation
Rose Family Chair in Supportive Care
Professor, Departments of Health Policy, Management and
Evaluation; Public Health Sciences; and Anesthesia
University Health Network and University of Toronto
Toronto, Canada

**Murray W Enkin MD, FRCSC, FACOG,
DSc (hon), LLD (hon)**
Professor Emeritus; Departments of Obstetrics and Gynecology;
and Clinical Epidemiology and Biostatistics; McMaster University;
Hamilton, Ontario
Adjunct Professor, University of Toronto,
Toronto, Canada

Blackwell
Publishing

BMJ|Books

© 2007 Alejandro Jadad & Murray Enkin

Published by Blackwell Publishing

BMJ Books is an imprint of the BMJ Publishing Group Limited, used under licence
Blackwell Publishing, Inc., 350 Main Street, Malden, Massachusetts 02148-5020, USA
Blackwell Publishing Ltd, 9600 Garsington Road, Oxford OX4 2DQ, UK
Blackwell Publishing Asia Pty Ltd, 550 Swanston Street, Carlton, Victoria 3053, Australia

The right of the Author to be identified as the Author of this Work has been asserted in
accordance with the Copyright, Designs and Patents Act 1988.

First edition published 1998

Second edition published 2007

1   2007

Library of Congress Cataloging-in-Publication Data
Jadad, Alejandro R.

  Randomized controlled trials : questions, answers, and musings / Alejandro
R. Jadad, Murray W. Enkin – 2nd ed.
      p. ; cm.
  Rev ed. of: Randomised controlled trials / Alejandro R. Jadad. 1998.
  Includes bibliographical references and index.
  ISBN 978-1-4051-3266-4 (pbk. : alk. paper)
  1. Clinical trials. I. Enkin, Murray. II. Jadad, Alejandro R. Randomised
controlled trials. III. Title.
  [DNLM: 1. Randomized Controlled Trials. 2. Quality Control. W 20.5 J21r
2007]

  R853.C55J33 2007
  615.5072′4–dc22   2007002574

ISBN: 978-1-4051-3266-4

A catalogue record for this title is available from the British Library

Set in Meridien 9.25/12 pt by Charon Tec Ltd (A Macmillan Company), Chennai, India
Printed and bound in Singapore by Utopia Press Pte Ltd

Commissioning Editor: Mary Banks
Editorial Assistant: Victoria Pittman
Development Editor: Lauren Brindley
Production Controller: Rachel Edwards

For further information on Blackwell Publishing, visit our website:
http://www.blackwellpublishing.com

The publisher's policy is to use permanent paper from mills that operate a sustainable
forestry policy, and which has been manufactured from pulp processed using acid-free
and elementary chlorine-free practices. Furthermore, the publisher ensures that the text
paper and cover board used have met acceptable environmental accreditation standards.

Contents

Foreword

I first met Alex Jadad at "Closing the Loop", an international conference on evidence-based practice, in 1999. His talk was a lively and amusing journey through the perils and pitfalls of the world of randomized controlled trials (RCTs). Afterwards we found an immediate sympathy with each others' views. We both recognized the value of research and also the various conundrums that arose in the interface between research and practice. We also felt that there were issues we could pursue together. We exchanged books and papers and wondered what we could do next.

When I received it, the first edition of *Randomised Controlled Trials* was an eye opener for me. Its painstaking overview of the design, understanding and application of RCTs enumerated many of the pitfalls, possible biases, and faulty designs inherent in the process, while at the same time recognizing the potential importance of finding genuine evidence for improved practice. It made an explicit promise that there would be more to come.

My discussions with Alex centred on what we recognized as an implicit assumption in the book. It seemed to be saying that "if only" we could rid ourselves of our biases, if we could only be more careful about the random allocation, if only we could perfect the way we carry out and report our experiments, then we could come up with the appropriate and rational answers to our clinical questions.

It was this implicit assumption that we began to question. It maintained that the problem was in the methodology of clinical research, rather than in the nature of the world of health and illness. It presumed that underlying the apparent mess there was a deeper order that could be discovered through rigorous research, that an understanding of this deeper order would in turn provide us with appropriate clinical protocols. We felt that it was worth thinking about the possibility that the world of health and illness might not be as orderly as we had assumed. Although large areas of pathophysiology and many diseases lent themselves to this rational deterministic model, there might also be many clinical circumstances where the model might not apply.

In philosophical terms we could say that the issue might be *ontological* rather than *epistemological*: about the *nature* of reality rather than about *how* we know it. For Alex it was a problem related to the realities of medical practice – how health professionals interacted with patients and how various factors influenced the interventions they made. Alex often spoke about his father, who was a particularly talented GP in South America. Alex thought of him as a model practitioner. His gift for understanding the needs of his patients and long experience in the use of a very limited number of drugs resulted in a noteworthy success in keeping his patients healthy.

Alex introduced me to Murray Enkin, his co-author for this second edition. Murray was an obstetrician who combined the experience of a sensitive caring practitioner, like Alex's father, with a strong commitment to providing a basis of evidence for good practice. They had met in Oxford where they had both been deeply involved in the evidence-based movement. The three of us, with like-minded colleagues, later initiated the Clinamen Collaboration to explore other models for thinking about health and health care.

We found the distinction between "simple" "complicated" and "complex" useful in our discussions. Where the problem is simple, there are often pre-tested solutions that are universally applicable – something like recipes for baking a cake, or straightforward clinical protocols that had few exceptions. Much medical practice is like this. It is scientifically based, well tested and lends itself to straightforward replicable recipes, and provides a firm basis for treating simple infections, inflammations, cuts and bruises.

More intricate problems are similarly solvable, but may require more complicated protocols. They need many more "recipes" strung together, and more technical expertise. Kidney transplant surgery, for example, requires a highly skilled surgeon, whose expertise will improve with experience. It also requires teamwork with other disciplines, varied but replicable facilities and resources. With each repetition the process is refined, understanding is increased, and results become more predictable.

Complex problems, like chronic illnesses and multi-system disease, are entirely different. They are not standardizable, but rather depend more on each individual case and context. The example of raising a second child is often used to make this point. Although some formulae fit all children, many do not. The approaches that worked for one's first child are only occasionally applicable to the second. Similarly, results of clinical interventions for complex problems may be impossible to predict. Few patients are alike, and even the same patient can respond differently at different times. Research is useful and instructive, but is not a substitute for clinical sensitivity to the unique situation of each individual patient.

This second edition takes into account the complexity of some areas of health care. Although it continues to recognize the importance of more stringent procedures and better experimental design, it now acknowledges that these will not be sufficient to solve the problems associated with the use of RCTs in practice. The musings added to each chapter explore what might be further needed to change the nature of the research enterprise, to allow a wider and richer source of evidence in the interplay between patients, research results and medical interventions.

Just as the first edition of this book was ground-breaking during the beginnings of evidence-based practice, this edition suggests many new possibilities and approaches to improved research for practice. From my perspective, I see several places where Jadad and Enkin begin to explore these issues.

In the case of chronic care, the role of the patient is especially important in searching for ongoing ways of coping with and treating a constellation of illnesses. The things that help are often discovered by patients and their families. Only they, not health professionals, can tell from their experience how and when foods are best taken, how hands-on care is properly applied, the subtle side effects of various medications and ways to avoid them. This is not merely to democratize medicine, but to recognize that useful interventions can be gathered from the kind of self-care that is part and parcel of chronic disease management. Increasingly useful self-help groups associated with various conditions pass on useful information of this kind. Experimental validation of these "tips" requires a different kind of attention and special methods.

In the current state of the health system, with its great emphasis on instrumental diagnosis, measurable and replicable results, the fact that not every aspect of care is susceptible to quantitative evidence can lead to scepticism about the entire enterprise. The widespread belief that if we can't measure it, it does not exist can lead to a sense of nihilism: This is clearly not warranted.

Let me go back to the example of raising a second child. The fact that there are not clear protocols for all interactions is hardly a basis for nihilism. We can cope perfectly well; we can benefit from the experience of the first child, and we can use some procedures that we have used before. But because each child is a complex individual we must pay special attention to the differences among different children, and follow their lead. Our knowledge and experience coupled with our capacity to respond to individual situations is the way forward, and allows us to maintain our optimism.

The same is true with health care interventions. We must deepen our understanding of the nature of the interaction between health professionals and patients, and recognize its richness and its potential to deal with the complexities and uncertainties that always have and will continue to confront this interaction in the future. This book is a big step in this direction.

Sholom Glouberman, PhD

Philosopher in Residence, Baycrest Centre for Geriatric Care
Associate Scientist, Kunin-Lunenfeld Applied Research Unit
Adjunct Professor, McGill University and University of Toronto Fellow,
The Change Foundation Toronto, Ontario, Canada

Preface to the first edition

Around 600 BC, Daniel of Judah conducted what is probably the earliest recorded clinical trial. He compared the health effects of a vegetarian diet with those of a royal Babylonian diet over a ten day period.[1] Despite the dramatic findings of the study, over 4 centuries elapsed before publication of the results. The trial had obvious deficiencies by contemporary methodologic standards (allocation bias, ascertainment bias, confounding by Divine intervention),[2] but the publication has remained influential for over two millennia.

Other controlled clinical studies with methodologic weaknesses but important effects on practice have been undertaken during the ensuing centuries. Ambrose Paré (1514–1564), in an unplanned experiment, found that applying a soothing 'digestive medicament' to battle wounds produced better results than the traditional practice of cauterizing wounds with boiling oil.[3] Inoculation to prevent smallpox became popular after Maitland conducted a trial upon six Newgate convicts in 1721,[3] although the numbers treated and the precision of the trial were not adequate to give a fair picture of the effects of the procedure. Jenner published his famous studies on vaccination at the end of the eighteenth century, based on 10 and 14 persons. Appalled by the ravages of scurvy among ships crews on long voyages, in 1747 James Lind conducted a comparative trial of the most promising scurvy cures, using as subjects 12 sick seamen on board the Salisbury at sea. 'The most sudden and visible good effects were perceived from the use of the oranges and lemons.' The British Navy did not supply lemon juice to its ships until 1795.[3]

The nineteenth century saw many major advances. Probably the most sophisticated trial of a preventive type was a before/after study conducted by Ignaz Semmelweis in 1847. He noted that maternal mortality was much higher among women delivered by physicians and medical students, who were in frequent contact with cadavers at autopsies, than among women delivered by pupil midwives. After considering various hypotheses he reasoned that 'the cadaveric particles clinging to the hands are not entirely removed by the ordinary method of washing the hands', and introduced the practice of more thorough washing and disinfectant.[4] Maternal mortality among the doctor-delivered mothers dropped by 50 per cent in the subsequent six months, although still not to as low a level as that achieved by the midwives.

Credit for the modern randomized trial is usually given to Sir Austin Bradford Hill. The historic MRC trials on streptomycin for pulmonary tuberculosis[5] are rightly regarded as a landmark that ushered in a new era of medicine. Their influence on the science of therapeutic evaluation was strengthened because the charismatic Hill followed up that work up with lectures and articles[6] reinforcing his message. Since Hill's pioneer achievement randomized trial methodology has been increasingly accepted, and the number of randomized controlled trials reported has grown exponentially. The current issue of the Cochrane Library[7] lists 158,065 such trials, and they have become the underlying basis for what is currently called 'evidence-based medicine'. The concept has rightly been hailed as a paradigm shift in our approach to clinical decision making.[8]

It is not, however, the first such paradigm shift. A similar scientific revolution was hailed more than a century and a half ago, by the editor of the American Journal of Medical Sciences in 1836, in his introduction to an article which he considered to be 'one of the most important medical works of the present century, marking the start of a new era in science'. It was 'the first formal exposition of the results of the *only true method of investigation* (emphasis added) in regard to the therapeutic value of remedial agents'. The article that evoked such effusive praise was the French study on bloodletting in the treatment of pneumonia by PCA Louis.[9,10]

At that time blood-letting was the almost universally accepted 'proper' method of treating pneumonia. Louis used the quintessential Baconian approach, of gathering vast amounts of data, which allowed him to make comparisons and systematically investigate the efficacy of treatments. His conclusion from that study was a bombshell; that the apparent efficacy of bleeding for pneumonia is a mere therapeutic illusion. His contribution to clinical epidemiology was to base recommendations for therapy on the results of collective experience, rather than on limited individual experience, tradition, or theory.

Louis's approach, and his evangelical zeal in promoting his methods created considerable controversy. He attracted many foreign disciples, including Oliver Wendell Holmes and William Osler who made their mentor's work available to American readers. He also attracted strong opposition, and his work was mired in controversy. His opponents were numerous and vociferous. 'The physician called to treat a sick man is not an actuary advising a company to accept or deny risks, but someone who must deal with a specific individual at a vulnerable moment'. 'Averages could not help and might even confuse the practising physician as he struggles to apply general rules to a specific case.' Practising physicians were unwilling to hold their decisions in abeyance till their therapies received numerical approbation, nor were they prepared to discard therapies validated by both tradition and their own experience on account of somebody else's numbers.[10]

Although doubtless they arose partly from an innate resistance to change, and partly from misguided self-interest, the arguments against a widespread application of the so-called numerical approach stemmed largely from a lack of understanding of its intent. When both practitioners and public finally became aware that collective experience enhanced, rather than replaced, the clinical skills of the individual physician, Louis' numerical approach became the basis of medical research and literature until the midpoint of this century. It was by no means a panacea, but was an enormous step on the way towards more effective health care.

The arguments heard against the numerical approach in the last century are remarkably similar to those used against evidence-based medicine today. Worries are still being expressed that evidence-based medicine confuses statistics with reality, results in a loss of clinical freedom, and ignores the importance of clinical experience and of individual values.[11] These concerns stem from the mistaken belief that the proponents of evidence-based medicine claim a multicentre double blind placebo controlled randomized trial to be the only way to answer a therapeutic question. This, despite the fact that Austin Bradford Hill himself said 'Any belief that the controlled trial is the only way would mean not that the pendulum had swung too far, but that it had come right off its hook'.[12] Evidence-based medicine is simply the conscientious and judicious use of the current best evidence from clinical care research to guide health care decisions. It is another enormous step towards more effective health care. No more, and no less.

One reason for the sometimes expressed opposition to evidence-based medicine is a lack of understanding of the meaning of a randomized trial. This failure of understanding is not due to a paucity of information; there is a vast literature about randomized trials, their purpose, their methodology, their limitations. Unfortunately, much of that literature has been incomplete, has been biassed, or has been couched in impenetrable jargon. It is not surprising that it has often been misinterpreted.

That is why this book is so welcome. It is written in clear, explicit, and understandable language, for those who use, would like to use, or should use, the results of randomized trials. It provides an accurate and comprehensive description of the randomized trial, its importance, when (and when not to) do a trial, how to interpret the results, when (and when not to) translate the results into health care decisions. It is a book to read, reflect on, learn from, use, and enjoy.

Murray W. Enkin
Dundas, 17 March 1998

References

1. Book of Daniel. In: *The Holy Bible.*
2. Grimes D. Clinical research in ancient Babylon: methodologic insights from the book of Daniel. *Obstetrics and Gynecology* 1995;86:1031–1034.
3. Bull BP. The historical development of clinical therapeutic trials. *Journal of Chronic Diseases* 1959;10:218–243.
4. Semmelweis IF. *The Etiology, the Concept, and the Prophylaxis of Childbed Fever* (1861). Translated and edited by Carter KC, University of Wisconsin Press, 1983.
5. Daniels M, Hill AB. Chemotherapy of pulmonary tuberculosis in young adults: an analysis of the combined results of three medical research council trials. *British Medical Journal* 1952;May 31:1162–1168.
6. Hill AB. The clinical trial. *New England Journal of Medicine* 1952; 247:113–119.
7. *The Cochrane Library* 1998. Disk issue 1.
8. Guyatt G, Evidence-based Medicine Working Group. Evidence-based medicine: a new approach to teaching the practice of medicine. *Journal of American Medical Association* 1992;268:2420–2425.
9. Louis PCA. Researches into the effects of blood-letting in some inflammatory diseases and on the influence of tartarized antimony and vesication in pneumonitis. *American Journal of Medical Sciences* 1836;18:102–111 (cited in Rangachari 1997).
10. Rangachari PK. Evidence-based medicine: old French wine with a new Canadian label? *Journal of the Royal Society of Medicine* 1997; 90:280–284.

11. Charlton BG. Restoring the balance: evidence-based medicine put in its place. *Journal of Evaluation in Clinical Practice* 1997;3:87–98.
12. Hill AB. Heberden oration, 1965. Reflections on the controlled trial. *Annals of Rheumatic Diseases* 1966;25:107–113.

Acknowledgments

We have so many people to thank. First (rather than the more usual 'last but not least') our families, whose unstinting love has meant so much to us: Martha Garcia whose support and constructive criticism helped Alex maintain his busy academic life and be part of a happy family; and Eleanor Enkin who provided not only valuable library research, but also perceptive comments, meals, cookies, ice cream, and needed hugs to sustain us. And we thank our children: Alia and Tamen; Susie, Nomi, Jane, and Randy; and Enkin grandchildren: Adam, Yoni, Daniel, Simon, Hannah, Shlomo, and Sura, who make it all worthwhile.

We appreciate the help of Dijana Vasic, who enabled Alex to set aside the time needed to make this an enjoyable project. We thank Lisa Askie for keeping the project alive until it could take off; Sholom Glouberman for opening up our minds to the complexity of health care; Charlie Goldsmith for detailed feedback on the first edition after its publication; and Kirstin Borgerson for her constructive criticism on bias. We are also grateful to those who helped, and were acknowledged in the first edition of this book, which made this second edition possible.

We thank the literary sources, including Lucretius and Austin Bradford Hill to whom we dedicated this book, and Archie Cochrane, Ivan Illich, Bruno Latour, and Mark Twain, who (among so many others) forced us to rethink many of our most cherished assumptions.

Finally, although most must remain unnamed, we thank our personal mentors, living and dead, never to be forgotten, who inspired us and taught us so much. The few that we name include George Browman, Beatriz Bechara de Borge, Iain Chalmers, Tom Chalmers, Mary Gospodarowicz, Marc Keirse, Mario Ruiz, Arturo Morillo, David Naylor, Bill Silverman, and Dave Sackett. They may not approve of all that we say in this book, but we are sure they will applaud our attempts to transcend the boundaries of conventional wisdom. They taught us that it is always healthy to challenge authority, especially our own.

Acknowledgments from the first edition

I would like to express my gratitude to all those, now anonymous, who asked me most of the questions that provided the structure of this book.

I would also like to thank a group of special people who have contributed significantly to my education as a clinician, researcher and teacher over the past 10 years. During my training in Colombia, Mario Ruiz exerted great influence on my research life, introduced me to the joy of clinical research and taught me the indelible meaning of the word mentor. German Parra showed me, for the first time, how research evidence can be integrated into clinical decisions, and Pedro Bejarano encouraged me, selflessly, to develop my research career abroad.

In England, Henry McQuay showed me the power of RCTs in health care and provided me with unprecedented conditions to nurture my curiosity and to speed up the development of my research skills. Iain Chalmers introduced me to systematic reviews and exemplified the meaning of collaboration. Chris Glynn showed me that busy clinicians can be researchers, provide humane patient care and have a rich personal life beyond medicine. His continuous challenges encouraged me to see the limitations of research evidence to guide health care decisions and motivated many of my efforts to overcome them. Clive Hahn encouraged me to write this book and Mary Banks, Senior Commissioning Editor (Books) at the BMJ Publishing Group made sure that it happened.

This book would have been much different without the influence of many of my colleagues at McMaster University. Some of them deserve special mention. I owe a lot to George Browman, who created the opportunity for me to come to Canada, expanded my research horizons, helped me to recognize the value of the research process and other types of information, and gave me unconditional support to develop my own agenda. I would also like to thank Brian Haynes, for re-reinforcing my notion of mentorship, and for helping me understand the need to integrate research evidence with the values, preferences and circumstances of the decision-makers. Geoff Norman introduced me to the principles of cognitive and social psychology, opened my eyes to the limitations of human inference, encouraged me to focus the book on users of research, and challenged me continuously to recognize the barriers to the practice of evidence-based decision-making created by our human nature.

For advice on matters academic or personal, I have turned repeatedly to Murray and Eleanor Enkin, my favorite couple. My family and I feel immensely privileged to call them friends. We owe them a great deal for the warmth with which they have welcomed us into their lives, for their wisdom, and for their kind but always-candid advice. Murray read each of the chapters of this book, and gave me invaluable advice on both content and structure. Each contact with Murray and Eleanor, regardless of whether it centres on academic, family or cultural issues, is always a rich learning experience.

I would also like to express my gratitude to those who gave their time to me generously to help put this book together. Tracey Hillier, Geoff Norman and Iain Chalmers provided very constructive comments on the initial outline of the book. Susan Marks read, patiently, each of the chapters of the book, always giving me friendly and highly professional suggestions to improve their readability and structure. Judi Padunsky proofread most of the chapters, supported my communication with the publishers and organized the references for the whole book. Laurie Kendry and Mary Gauld read several chapters of the book and provided valuable input. Comments by Brian Haynes and Geoff Norman contributed enormously to the last chapter.

I owe more to my family than to anyone else. My extended family in South America showed me, from a very early age, the meaning of teamwork, unconditional support and trust. I could have not possibly written this book without Martha, my wife and best friend. Once more, her love, support and constructive criticism have helped me maintain a busy academic life and be part of a happy family. Finally, I would like to give special thanks to my daughters Alia and Tamen, for giving a new meaning to all I do.

Alejandro (Alex) R. Jadad

Introduction to the second edition

Why a second edition?

The value of randomized trials was already established in 1998 when Alex Jadad, as a newly established clinical researcher, wrote the first edition of this book. He wrote it to fill a need he had himself felt, for a 'comprehensive source of basic information about the underlying principles, methodology, and role of trials in health care decisions'. The methodology of RCTs had matured, there was a burgeoning acceptance of their value, but they were still not as widely understood or utilized as they should have been. He felt somewhat as the pioneer Bradford Hill must have felt in 1951, when he carefully explained the new concepts of the clinical trial, 'the highly organized and efficiently controlled therapeutic trial of new remedies'. If these had been properly used, he said 'we should have gained a fairly precise knowledge of the place of individual methods of therapy in disease, and our efficiency as doctors would have been enormously enhanced.'[1]

It did not take Bradford Hill long to recognize that clinical research was far more complex than he had originally thought. Less than 20 years after the first randomized trial[2] he noted that 'the present quality and scale of clinical trials are an increasingly serious bottle neck in the development and effective use of drugs', and 'there is a blind acceptance of double-blind trials without a critical evaluation of their short-comings and their ability to mislead as well as to lead'.

The need for a 'comprehensive source of basic information about the underlying principles, methodology, and role of trials in health care decisions' has remained unchanged as a new generation of researchers and clinicians have entered the health care field. What has changed since the first edition of this book is not randomized trials *per se*, but our recognition of the complexity of the world in which they are conceived, funded, carried out, disseminated, understood, used, and abused.

It is these wider questions that prompted our decision to provide a new edition of *Randomized Controlled Trials*. Randomized trials have not only influenced health care, they have also influenced and been influenced by the local and global health care environment of which they are an integral part. We felt that it was time for a new look.

Why a new co-author?

Not really new. We have been close colleagues even before the first edition was started. Murray reviewed each chapter of *Randomised Controlled Trials* while it was under construction, and wrote the foreword to that edition. Although there is a 40-year difference in age between us, and we come from vastly different backgrounds, during more than a decade we have recognized the extent to which our paths and thinking have converged. We first noticed this in Oxford with our mutual interest in systematic reviews, and confirmed it at McMaster University as we became painfully aware of the pitfalls of over reliance on quantitative evidence and its limited influence on health care. During the past 5 years, our focus has been more on the value of rhetoric, information and communication technologies, complex systems, and the importance of effective communication in the health system.

Over the years, we have grown together in our understanding, have worked together on a variety of projects, and mutually reinforced our views on clinical evidence. We are happy to share our expanding vision of randomized trials in this new edition.

What is new in the second edition?

Those who offer or use health care still need a convenient and understandable source for basic information about randomized trials. Some chapters in the first edition provided this clearly, and in these, except for some newer and more current references, we have made only minor changes. Other chapters, however, have required more significant modifications, to incorporate the broader insights that have been gained during this period, as randomized trials have grown exponentially both in their number and their influence.

We have maintained the question and answer format that was so positively received by readers of the first edition, and kept the text free of formulas and unnecessary jargon. We have added a chapter on the ethics of randomized trials, which are not as simple and straightforward as we used to think that they were; we felt that ethical considerations are every bit as important as methodology, and it is just as important to make them explicit.

Each chapter in the new edition ends with a section we call 'Our Musings'. In this section we go beyond the evidence or citations, and sometimes even beyond orthodox correctness to share our thoughts and concerns on the chapter topic with our readers. It has been exhausting, strenuous, and fun. We have learned more about randomized trials, about each topic, and about ourselves than we had believed possible. We hope that each reader will do their own musings on these topics, and, like the alchemists of old, transmute them into their personal elixir.

References

1. Hill, AB. The clinical trial. *British Medical Bulletin* 1951;7:278–282.
2. Hill, AB. Heberden oration, 1965: reflections on the controlled trial. *Annals of Rheumatic Disease* 1966;25:107–113.

Introduction to the first edition

This is a book for busy readers who need, wish or have to understand the basic principles of randomized controlled trials (RCTs) and their role in health care decisions. It is my best effort to fill a gap in the literature that was not able to fill with any single source during the past 15 years.

In the 1980s, as a medical student, intern, resident, and novice researcher, I could not find a single source that could help me really understand what RCTs were about, their strengths and limitations, and how to use them while making health care decisions. During that decade, I had to rely on many sources, most of which were written in a language that was difficult for me to understand, that presented information in formats that I could not adapt to my busy life or to my rapidly changing needs. I attributed my failed attempts to find a single, easy-to-read source of basic information to the fact that I was in Colombia, a developing country where it was often difficult to access the biomedical literature.

In 1990 I moved to England, where I spent 5 years as a research fellow, as a practicing clinician and as a graduate student. At the beginning of this period, the need for a good source of information to fill my most basic knowledge gaps intensified. My colleagues at Oxford were seasoned trialists. They not only designed and analyzed their own trials, but also criticized, quite strongly, trials done by others. As I did not want to bother my colleagues with basic questions (or to sound dumb), I started looking, again, for a source of information that could meet my most immediate needs. To my surprise, I could not find one. I started to list my questions and decided to get answers as soon as possible, from as many sources as necessary. I spent vast amounts of time (and not insignificant amounts of money) trying to get small pieces of information from different books, most of which targeted doers of research, not users. I also started asking for key references from colleagues, and tracked down articles mentioned by speakers at conferences or included in the reference lists of the articles I was collecting from other sources. As my list of questions grew, so did my list of references and contacts. After a while, I felt more comfortable to talk to my colleagues about trials, started to design and lead some trials myself, and was invited to coordinate journal club sessions, where the work of others was rigorously appraised. Two years after my arrival in Oxford, one of my RCTs was published in The Lancet! This experience, however, created another set of challenges. Colleagues started to invite me to give lectures on pain research and trial design. I found myself under a different type of pressure. I had the opportunity, for the first time, to transmit to others what I had learnt. I began to feel confident about acknowledging my own uncertainties and knowledge gaps. People seemed to like my presentations and I started to receive invitations to give lectures. It did not take me long to realize that the attendees were asking similar questions from lecture to lecture, and that those questions were similar to those I had listed before. I started recording the questions and made every effort to address them during each successive lecture. As a result, the original questions gave way to new questions. Soon, some of the new questions from the audience started to coincide with my own questions at the time. I kept adding the new questions to my list for the 5 years I was in England. The questions I collected, approximately 100, form the backbone of this book.

In 1992, I was accepted as a graduate student at the University of Oxford and started to work on a thesis on meta-analysis of randomized trials in pain relief. As part of my thesis work, I coded over 15,000 citations and created a database with over 8,000 RCTs. I also led the development of what is regarded by many as the first validated tool to appraise the quality of RCTs, and created new statistical methods to combine data from different RCTs addressing the same topic. When I tried to use the newly developed methods to answer clinical important questions, I realized that despite having thousands of RCTs at my fingertips, relevant data were often unavailable or poorly reported. I also started to formulate questions about RCTs that had not yet been answered at all and became interested in the design of methodological studies to answer them. During this period, I started to meet people who shared my interest in addressing unanswered methodological questions. Most of them had published a number of studies that looked at the RCT as the subject of research, rather than as the research tool. Through my interaction with this different breed of researchers and their work, and my own methodological studies, I became aware of how vulnerable the RCT can be to bias, imprecision, irrelevance and politics at all stages of its development and in all areas of health care.

Soon after I completed my thesis work, I moved to McMaster University, where I was expecting to have a quieter time, as a postdoctoral fellow, applying all my new knowledge on RCTs and systematic reviews, and exploring ways to involve consumers in health decisions. I was pleasantly surprised. I found lots of exciting work on RCTs and systematic reviews at McMaster; but through my interaction with my new colleagues, I became aware of the profound impact that factors other than evidence from RCTs can have on clinical decisions and health outcomes. Under their influence, I began to grasp the complexity of human-human, human-information, human-technology and information-technology interactions. My world became richer, and once again I faced new challenges. I started to look on RCTs as powerful but vulnerable tools that can make important but small contributions to a large puzzle with many pieces that are continuously changing their shape, size and patterns.

At that point, writing a book on RCTs moved from being a relatively easy task to a daunting one. I almost turned down the offer to write this book. It took me more than a year to draft the first chapter, and more than a year to complete the book.

At first, I was tempted to target the book to both doers (i.e., fellow researchers and academics) and users (i.e., clinicians, policy makers and managers, and if brave enough, consumers) of research. After drafting many tables of contents, I realized that trying to meet the needs of such a diverse group at the same time would be a mistake. After some deliberation, I decided to produce an introductory guide for busy readers. Primarily, this book is aimed at clinicians, young researchers and trainees in any health profession. Nevertheless, I hope that health planners, managers, journal editors, peer-reviewers, journalists, members of consumer advocacy groups and even seasoned researchers could also find it relevant and useful.

The book is divided into eight chapters, and addresses 100 questions with short answers and key references. The first five chapters focus on individual trials and include definitions of key elements of trials, descriptions of different types of RCTs and sources of bias, discussions of different approaches to quality assessment, and tips on trial reporting and interpretation. The sixth chapter focuses on groups of RCTs and includes discussions on different types of reviews, meta-analyses and clinical practice guidelines. The seventh chapter addresses the role of RCTs in health care decisions, their relationship with other types of information, values, preferences and circumstances. This chapter also introduces the basic principles of evidence based decision-making and highlights its strengths and limitations. The last chapter describes 'my wish list'. In it, I highlight what I think are the most important barriers to the optimal use of RCTs in health care, and propose some strategies that could be used to overcome them.

Writing each of the chapters of this book was an extraordinary experience, full of challenges and lessons. The main challenge was to ensure that I could complete the book without affecting my family life or my responsibilities as a new faculty member. The only way in which I could do this was by modifying my sleep pattern. This book was written, essentially, from 11 PM to 2 AM or from 4 AM to 6 AM. Working at these hours gave me more time than I had had in years to think about trials and to put together my thoughts without interruptions. Putting each chapter together forced me to be concise and to use easy-to-read language to describe even the most complex aspects of RCTs. I made every effort to describe the key elements and implications of RCTs without statistics, and in a way that would appeal to busy readers. Each chapter created new questions and opened new avenues for me to explore. During each session I struggled, continuously, to keep the balance between the need to describe the basic elements of RCTs and the urge to express my concerns and expectations about health care research as a whole.

In sum, I did my best to provide you with an enjoyable, balanced, useful and broad view of RCTs and their role in health care. I hope I succeeded.

Alejandro (Alex) R. Jadad
Dundas, 11 June 1998

CHAPTER 1

Randomized controlled trials: the basics

What is a randomized controlled trial?

The randomized controlled trial (RCT) is one of the simplest, most powerful, and revolutionary tools of research.[1,2] In essence, the RCT is a study in which people are allocated 'at random' to receive one of several interventions.

The people who take part in RCTs (the *'study population'*) are called *'participants'* or, irritatingly to some people, *'subjects'*. Participants do not have to be patients, as a study can be conducted in healthy volunteers, in relatives of patients, in members of the general public, in communities, or institutions. The people who design and carry out the study and analyze the results are called the *'investigators'* (The interventions are sometimes called *'clinical maneuvers'*, and include varied actions such as preventive strategies, diagnostic tests, screening programs, and treatments.) For instance, if we are conducting a study in which patients with rheumatoid arthritis who are randomized to receive either ibuprofen or a new drug (let us call it 'perfectafen') for the relief of pain, we and our colleagues would be the investigators; the participants the patients with rheumatoid arthritis; and the interventions ibuprofen and perfectafen.

Typically, RCTs seek to measure and compare different events called *'outcomes'* that are present or absent after the participants receive the interventions. Because the outcomes are quantified (or measured), RCTs are regarded as *'quantitative'* studies. In our hypothetical RCT comparing ibuprofen and perfectafen, for instance, the investigators could select pain as the main outcome, measuring it in terms of the number of patients who achieve complete relief 1 week after starting treatment.

Because RCTs are used to compare two or more interventions, they are considered *'comparative'* studies. Usually, one of the interventions is regarded as a standard of comparison or *'control'*, and the group of participants who receive it is called the *'control group'*. This is why RCTs are referred to as randomized *'controlled'* trials. The control can be conventional practice, a placebo, or no intervention at all. The other groups are called the *'experimental'* or the *'treatment'* groups. In our example, the experimental group is the group that receives 'perfectafen' (the new treatment) and the control group is the one that receives ibuprofen, the standard treatment. Some trials could compare different doses of the same medication, or different ways of administering the intervention as part of either the experimental or control groups.

RCTs are *'experiments'* because the investigators can influence the number and the type of interventions, as well as the regimen (amount, route, and frequency) with which the interventions are applied to the participants. This is in contrast to other types of studies, called *'observational'*, in which the events are not influenced by the investigators. We describe these, briefly, in Chapter 7.

In summary, RCTs are quantitative comparative controlled experiments in which a group of investigators study two or more interventions in a series of individuals who are randomly *'allocated'* (chosen) to receive them.

What does random allocation mean?

Random allocation means that participants are assigned to one of the study groups by chance alone.[3] The decision as to which group they will be in is not determined or influenced by the investigators, the clinicians, or the study participants.

Despite its simplicity, the principle of randomization is often misunderstood by clinicians, researchers, journal reviewers, and even journal editors. Methods to allocate participants according to date of birth (odd or even years), the number of their hospital records, the date in which they are invited to participate in the study (odd or even days), or alternately into the different study groups should not be regarded as really generating random allocation sequences. Although if no one cheats, these 'non-random' or 'quasi-random' studies could produce well-balanced groups, knowledge of the group to which a participant is destined can affect the decision about whether to enter him or her into the trial. This could bias the results of the whole trial.[4]

What is the purpose of random allocation?

By allocating the participants randomly, the characteristics of the participants are likely to be similar across groups at the start of the comparison (also called '*baseline*'). By keeping the groups '*balanced at baseline*' (as similar as possible at the beginning of the study) the investigators will be more able to isolate and quantify the impact of the interventions they are studying, while minimizing effects from other factors that could influence the outcomes (these are called '*confounding factors*').

Either known or unknown factors not related directly to the interventions can influence the outcomes of a study. It is fairly easy to match the groups for possible confounding factors, when we know about them. The groups can be kept balanced without randomization as long as all the possible confounding factors have been measured. For example, if 'perfectafen' is evaluated in a retrospective study, the investigators could select a group of patients who received ibuprofen and who took antacids that would match the proportion of patients who took antacids and received 'perfectafen'. But we cannot match groups for factors about which we are not aware. The value of randomization is that if it is done properly, it reduces the risk of serious imbalance in important unknown as well as known factors that could influence the clinical course of the participants. No other study design allows investigators to balance these unknown factors.

The risk of imbalance among the groups is not abolished completely, even if the allocation is perfectly randomized. There are many types of bias that can influence the composition and characteristics of the study groups, even before a trial begins and long after it is completed. We discuss these biases in Chapter 3.

How can randomization be achieved?

We can generate random sequences of allocation in several different ways. Regardless of the method used, investigators should follow two principles: first, they must define the rules that will govern allocation; and second, they should follow those rules strictly throughout the whole study.

In principle, the simplest methods to generate random sequences of allocation are 'flipping a coin' (for studies with two groups) and 'rolling a die' (for studies with two or more groups), although they are rarely used because they do not leave an audit trail.

Investigators can also use 'random number tables' to generate the sequences. Random number tables contain a series of numbers which occur equally often, and that are arranged in a random (therefore unpredictable) fashion. The numbers usually have two or more digits. The use of a random number table forces investigators to decide the correspondence between the numbers and the groups (e.g. odd corresponding to group A and even to group B; or numbers from 01 to 33 to group A, from 34 to 66 to group B, and from 67 to 99 to group C). Then they have to select the starting point in the table (i.e. the beginning, the end, or any point in the middle of the table marked by a pencil dropped with the eyes closed) and the direction in which the table will be read (e.g. upward or downward). If the numbers in the table contain more than two digits, the investigators have to select the position of the numbers that will determine allocation. For example, if the table contains numbers with four digits (e.g. 2314, 5781, 6703, 8092), the investigators can choose, for example, the last two digits, or the first two, or the first and third. The crucial point is to first define the procedure, and then, once the procedure is defined, do not modify it at any point during the study.

A similar set of numbers may be generated by a computer that is programmed to do so, or by most scientific calculators. The procedures and rules that the investigators must follow are identical to those described for the random number tables.

Regardless of the method the investigators use to generate random sequences of allocation, the number and characteristics of the participants allocated to each of the study groups will probably differ (although slightly) at any given point during the study.[3] To minimize these differences, investigators can use some strategies known as *'restricted* (or *block*) randomization', or *'stratified randomization'*.

Restricted randomization is used to keep the numbers of participants in all the study groups as close as possible. It is achieved by creating 'blocks' of sequences that will ensure that the same number of participants will be allocated to the study groups within each block. For example, in a study with three groups (A, B, and C), the investigators can create six blocks: ABC, ACB, BAC, BCA, CAB, and CBA.

Stratified randomization is used to keep the 'characteristics' of the participants (e.g. age, weight, or functional status) as similar as possible across the study groups. To achieve this, investigators must first identify factors (or 'strata') that are known to be related to the outcome of the study. Once these factors are identified, the next step is to produce a separate block randomization scheme for each factor to ensure that the groups are balanced within each stratum.

On occasion, investigators may not desire the same number of participants in each of the study groups and can decide to allocate unequal numbers to each group, while preserving the homogeneity of the distribution of the characteristics of the participants across the study groups. This is called *'weighted'* or *'unequal'* randomization. This type of randomization tends to be used by investigators who wish to expose fewer participants to the experimental group because of concerns about unexpected adverse events. In the example of ibuprofen versus perfectafen, the investigators may decide to allocate one patient to perfectafen for every four patients who receive ibuprofen.

Unfortunately, the methods of allocation in studies described as 'randomized' are sometimes poorly reported, and sometimes not reported at all, even when such studies are published in prominent journals.[5,6] Because of these poor descriptions, it is not possible to determine, on most occasions, whether the investigators used a proper method to generate random sequences of allocation. Also, even when the reports of studies described as randomized provide details of the methods of allocation, it has been shown that 5%–10% do not use methods that generate random sequences.[7,8] The reporting of randomization and other aspects of RCTs will be discussed in detail in Chapter 5.

What can be randomized in RCTs?

The most frequent unit of allocation in RCTs is individual people, either patients (the commonest) or caregivers (e.g. treating physicians or nurses). But other units can equally well be randomized to answer specific questions.

Sometimes it is more appropriate to randomize groups of people rather than individuals. This is known as *'cluster'* randomization. Examples of these clusters are hospitals, families, and geographic areas. Investigators frequently use this approach when the RCTs are designed to evaluate interventions that may affect more than one individual within a particular group (e.g. RCTs evaluating the effect of a videotape on smoking cessation on prison inmates, or the effects on parents following a policy of early discharge from hospital after childbirth). It is also used when the way in which the participants in one study group are treated or assessed is likely to modify the treatment or assessment of participants in other groups. This phenomenon is known as *'contamination'*. For example, contamination would be present in an RCT comparing the use of a booklet describing strategies to increase patient participation in treatment decisions versus conventional practice, if patients who have received the booklet shared it with patients who did not.

In other cases, investigators may decide to randomize not only individuals or groups of individuals, but also the order in which the measurements are obtained from each participant. For instance, in an RCT evaluating the effects of morphine on cancer pain, the investigators could randomize the order in which analgesia, adverse effects, and quality of life are assessed.

When are randomized trials needed?

Randomized trials are needed to determine the effects of a health care intervention when these effects are not absolutely clear from observational studies. The effects of some health care interventions, such as antibiotics for pneumonia, or Cesarean section for an obstructed labor, are so dramatic that no further testing is required. More often the effects are less dramatic and may be highly influenced by external factors. Small to moderate effects of interventions can be very important, if the health problem is serious or common.

How are RCTs used?

When reading a trial protocol or a report, it is always wise to consider the purpose of the trial. The theoretical purpose of an RCT is to promote health through a better understanding of the benefits or harms of one or more interventions. A well-conceived, well-performed RCT can inform, enhance, and sometimes change clinical practice or policy. Trials can help individual clinicians to guide their practice, and clinical communities to determine or modify practice patterns. They can provide patients and the public with the information to help them choose what they feel to be the best for them as individuals. Government agencies utilize RCTs for approval of drugs or devices. Insurance agencies, private or government, use them to determine which services or procedures warrant insurance coverage. Institutions can use them to make health policy decisions.

RCTs can, of course, also be used for other purposes. They may be carried out for career advancement or purely for curiosity. They may be funded by companies (most often pharmaceutical, but increasingly also the manufacturing of devices) for regulatory and marketing purposes. They also serve as a powerful form of rhetoric to convince skeptics and doubters, or to control trends that could be considered as too expensive or too disruptive.

How are trials managed and overseen?

Major attention is usually given to when and how RCTs are conceived, designed, and analyzed. All too often, however, too little attention is paid to the actual ongoing meticulous management and oversight of a clinical trial.

Ideally, all activities within a trial must be guided by a *'protocol'*, a document that outlines the research question, the rationale for the trial, and the systems that must be set up for recruitment of participants, randomization, data entry, filing, and analysis. These must be clearly established and understood by everyone concerned.

Trials are conducted by research teams led by someone known as the *'principal investigator'*, a person who is able to command the respect of fellow collaborators, other clinicians, and the rest of the trial management team. A key member of this team is the *'trial coordinator'*, the person responsible for the day-to-day management of the trial and who must be able to respond to the problems that inevitably arise. In addition to the principal investigator (usually known as the 'PI') and the coordinator, the team often includes research assistants, statisticians, data managers, administrative staff, and, increasingly, computer programmers. This team is responsible for ensuring the highest possible levels of quality during patient recruitment, data collection and analysis, and knowledge transfer.[9]

Collecting information and entering it on a computer is relatively simple. Ensuring that the data are valid and sensible is a complicated and detailed process. This often requires lateral thinking, flexibility, good communication, and a great deal of common sense.

The Internet is now playing a larger role in the management of trials, challenging the traditional roles of (and even the need for) each of the members of the management team. An increasing number of tools now allow posting of protocols on the World Wide Web, self-matching by potential trial participants, automatic computer-generated randomization codes, data entry and analysis, results reporting, and audit. Many of these tools are driven by commercial interests and are undergoing rapid transformation under the impetus for market dominance. Governments and academic groups as well are also starting to support the use of online tools. One of the main challenges in the foreseeable future will be to achieve standardized ways to handle each of the components of a trial online, to promote economies of scale, and efficient and equitable access and exchange of knowledge worldwide.

Can RCTs answer all questions related to health care interventions?

Although RCTs are considered 'the best of all research designs'[10] or 'the most powerful tool in modern clinical research'[11] they are by no means a panacea to answer all health care questions. There are many situations in which they are not feasible, necessary, appropriate, or sufficient to help solve important problems.

The term *'intervention'* is widely used in health care, but infrequently defined. On most occasions the term intervention refers to treatment. However, as we discussed at the beginning of this chapter, this term can be, and often is, used in a much wider sense, to include any health care element offered to the study participants that may have an effect on their health status. Examples include preventive strategies, screening programs, diagnostic tests, the setting in which health care is provided, or educational models. Some of these may be difficult or impossible to study with the methodology of an RCT.

Even when RCT evidence is available, it may not be sufficient to provide all the answers that clinicians, patients, or policy makers need.[12,13] In these cases, we may either require further trials, or use other types of studies to complement the information provided by available RCTs. We discuss other study designs and other types of information, with their advantages and disadvantages, in Chapter 7.

There are many questions for which RCTs are not appropriate. These are usually related to aspects of health care that cannot or should not be influenced by the investigators, such as issues related to the etiology, natural history of diseases, or when the outcomes of interest are adverse effects. It would be unethical and wrong, for instance, to design an RCT in which people would be randomized to smoke or not for decades to compare the prevalence of lung cancer between smokers and non-smokers.

In other circumstances, RCTs may not be worthwhile because of financial constraints, low compliance rates or high drop out rates, or long intervals between the interventions and the outcomes. It would not be possible to carry out an RCT to evaluate the effects of an intervention with very rare outcomes or with effects that take long periods of time to develop. In these cases, other study designs such as case–control studies or cohort studies are more appropriate.

Most RCTs focus on clinical questions and management of disease. Many of the major determinants of health or illness, such as absolute or relative poverty, social class, literacy, transportation or other infrastructure, are not amenable to medical interventions. RCTs can only answer questions for which quantitative results are applicable. A research focus on the types of problems that can be addressed by RCTs can divert our attention and resources from other, equally important health-related problems. Many things that really count cannot be counted.

It follows that before we start reading an RCT, or even searching for one, we should take into account that there are other study designs that may be more appropriate to answer our particular questions. In addition, one RCT in isolation, even when it is appropriate and perfectly designed, is unlikely to provide all the answers we need. We should consider the information provided by a single RCT as an important piece in a puzzle with many empty spaces. This information will have to be assessed and used in conjunction with other types of information (e.g. data from other RCTs or from other study designs, and our own experience), and the values and preferences of the people involved in the decisions, depending on the circumstances in which the decisions are being made.

Our musings

It is very difficult to convey, at the same time, the strengths of RCTs, the value that they have, the risks of over-reliance on them, or their abuse. These concepts swing back and forth as a pendulum. As one of the pioneers of controlled trials, Sir Austin Bradford Hill, put it 'when we think that RCTs can provide all the answers, that doesn't mean just that the pendulum has swung too far, but that it has swung completely off the hook'.[14]

Following the celebration of the 50th anniversary of modern trials, several articles drew attention to the way in which these powerful tools had been hijacked by special interest groups, reducing their ability to provide valid, precise, and relevant answers to important questions.[2,15,16] Since then, these warning calls have been reinforced by highly visible examples of misconduct among funders, policy makers, and researchers, as well as by articles and books by former editors of prominent journals about the current levels of corruption and unethical behavior that exists within the research engine that fuels the drug regulatory process.[17–19]

We now feel that there is an increasing polarization of views about RCTs, along a spectrum of views that ranges from those who put trials on the pedestal of the hierarchy of evidence to those who consider RCTs a dangerous distraction. At the dawn of the 21st century, as the complexity of most health care issues increases[20,21] we have come to realize that trials are valuable sources of knowledge, but not always the most important or even trustworthy ones. One of our greatest challenges will be to learn not only how to carry out scientifically sound and morally ethical RCTs, but why and when to do them.

References

1. Silverman WA, Chalmers I. Sir Austin Bradford Hill: an appreciation. *Controlled Clinical Trials* 1992;13:100–105.
2. Jadad AR, Rennie D. The randomized controlled trial gets a middle-aged checkup. *Journal of American Medical Association* 1998;279(4):319–320.
3. Altman DG. *Practical Statistics for Medical Research,* 2nd edition. London: Chapman & Hall, 2006.
4. Schulz KF. Subverting randomization in controlled trials. *Journal of American Medical Association* 1995;274:1456–1458.
5. Altman DG, Doré CJ. Randomisation and baseline comparisons in clinical trials. *Lancet* 1990;335:149–153.
6. Moher D, Fortin P, Jadad AR, Jüni P, Klassen T, Le Lorier J, Liberati A, Linde K, Penna A. Completeness of reporting of trials in languages other than English: implications for the conduct and reporting of systematic reviews. *Lancet* 1996;347:363–366.
7. Mosteller F, Gilbert JP, McPeek B. Reporting standards and research strategies for controlled trials: agenda for the editor. *Controlled Clinical Trials* 1980;1:37–58.
8. Evans M, Pollock AV. Trials on trial: a review of trials of antibiotic prophylaxis. *Archives of Surgery* 1984;119:109–113.
9. Farrell B. Efficient management of randomized trials: nature or nurture. *British Medical Journal* 2006;317:1236–1239.
10. Norman GR, Streiner DL. *Biostatistics: The Bare Essentials.* Hamilton: Decker, 2000. Smith R. The trouble with medical journals. London: Royal Society of Medicine Press, 2007.
11. Silverman WA. Gnosis and random allotment. *Controlled Clinical Trials* 1981;2:161–166.
12. Naylor CD. Grey zones of clinical practice: some limits to evidence-based medicine. *Lancet* 1995;345:840–842.
13. Freemantle N. Dealing with uncertainty: will science solve the problem of resource allocation in the UK NHS? *Social Sciences and Medicine* 1995;40:1365–1370.

14. Hill AB. Heberden Oration 1965: reflections on the controlled trial. *Annals of Rheumatic Diseases* 1965;25:107–113.
15. Horton R. The clinical trial: deceitful, disputable, unbelievable, unhelpful, and shameful – what next? *Controlled Clinical Trials* 2001;22:593–604.
16. Smith R. Medical journals and pharmaceutical companies: uneasy bedfellows. *British Medical Journal* 2003;326:1202–1205.
17. Angell M. *The Truth About the Drug Companies: How They Deceive Us and What to Do about It*, 1st edition. New York: Random House. 2004.
18. Kassirer JP. *On the Take: How Medicine's Complicity with Big Business Can Endanger Your Health*. USA: Oxford University Press, 2005.
19. Smith R. *The Trouble with Medical Journals*. Royal Society of Medicine Press. 2007.
20 Plsek PE, Greenhalgh T. The challenge of complexity in health care. *British Medical Journal* 2001;323:625–628.
21. www.healthandeverything.org (accessed December 22, 2006).

CHAPTER 2

Types of randomized controlled trials

Randomized controlled trials (RCTs) can be used to evaluate different types of interventions in different populations of participants, in different settings, and for different purposes. Once investigators ensure that allocation of participants to the study groups is random (necessary to call the study an RCT), they can design the study using strategies to match the characteristics of the interventions they want to study, the resources they have available, and their academic, political, marketing, or clinical motivations. Over the years, various jargon terms have been used to describe different types of RCTs. There is no single source with clear and simple definitions for all these terms, so this jargon may be difficult to understand for those who are starting their careers as clinicians or researchers.

In this chapter, we will describe the terms most frequently used to describe different types of RCTs, and do our best to classify them in a way that will be easy to follow, understand, and remember. Some of the terms apply specifically to RCTs, while others may also be applied to other study designs as well. Some terms are mutually exclusive, some overlap considerably, and some complement each other.

RCTs can be classified according to the aspects of the interventions they evaluate, the way in which the participants are exposed to the interventions, the units of analysis, the number of participants included in the study, whether the investigators and participants know which intervention is being assessed, and whether non-randomized individuals and participants' preferences are taken into account in the design of the study (Table 2.1).

RCTs that explore different aspects of the interventions

Depending on the aspects of the interventions that investigators want to evaluate, RCTs can be classified as efficacy, effectiveness, or equivalence trials; and as phase I, II, III, or IV trials.

Table 2.1 Types of RCTs

RCTs that explore different aspects of the interventions they evaluate
- Efficacy and effectiveness trials
- Equivalence trials
- Phase I, II, III, and IV trials

RCTs according to how the participants are exposed to the interventions
- Parallel trials
- Factorial design trials
- Cross-over trials

RCTs by unit of analysis
- Body part
- Individual
- Group (Institution, community, geographic, and location)

RCTs according to the number of participants
- Fixed to variable sample size
- N-of-1 trials to mega-trials

RCTs according to whether the investigators and participants know which intervention is being assessed
- Open trials
- Blinded (masked) trials

RCTs according to whether non-randomized individuals and participants' preferences are taken into account
- Zelen's design
- Comprehensive cohort design
- Wennberg's design

What is the difference between an efficacy and an effectiveness trial?

RCTs are often described in terms of whether they evaluate the *efficacy* or the *effectiveness* of an intervention. These two concepts are sometimes confused because of the similarity of their names.

The term *'efficacy'* refers to whether an intervention works in people who actually receive it.[1] An *efficacy trial* (sometimes referred to as an explanatory trial) aims to address the question of whether or not an intervention *can* work under optimal circumstances, and how. An efficacy trial is designed in such a way that the results are likely to yield a 'clean' evaluation of the intervention. To achieve this, the investigators set strict inclusion criteria that will produce highly homogeneous study groups. For instance, for an efficacy trial of the effects of a new anti-hypertensive drug they could decide to include only patients between 40 and 50 years of age, with no co-existing diseases. (A hypertensive patient who also had, for example, diabetes would not be eligible for inclusion.) They would also exclude those receiving other relevant interventions (such as beta-blockers).

The investigators will try to include only participants who will follow their instructions and who will actually receive the intervention. The extent to which study participants follow the instructions given by the investigators is called *compliance* or *adherence*. High compliance is easy to achieve when the administration of the interventions can be completely controlled by the investigators or by health professionals who are supportive of the study (e.g. an RCT comparing the effects of coronary artery bypass surgery and those of angioplasty in patients with unstable angina). Compliance is easier to achieve for trials of short duration. It is more difficult to achieve when the interventions are administered by the participants themselves, when the study has a long duration, and when the interventions have to be administered several times a day. Returning to the example of the anti-hypertensive drug previously discussed, compliance will depend on the extent to which the participants take the anti-hypertensive tablets as prescribed for the whole duration of the study. To make high compliance more likely, the investigators may choose to include only patients who have already shown high compliance in other studies or in preliminary tests.

Efficacy trials also tend to use placebos as controls, fixed regimens (such as 20 mg by mouth every 6 hours), long washout periods (if patients have been taking diuretics, for instance, those drugs will be stopped for a period of time long enough to ensure that they are 'washed out' of their bodies), intention-to-treat analysis (see Chapter 3), and focus on 'hard' outcomes (i.e. blood pressure recorded at specific times following a detailed and standardized process).

The term '*effectiveness*' refers to whether an intervention *does* work, rather than whether it *can* work. An *effectiveness trial* (sometimes called a *pragmatic* or *management* trial) typically evaluates an intervention with proven efficacy when it is offered to a heterogeneous group of people under ordinary clinical circumstances.[2] Effectiveness trials are designed to determine not only whether the intervention achieves specific outcomes, but also to describe all the consequences of its use, good and bad, for people to whom it has been offered, under circumstances mimicking clinical practice. To achieve this, effectiveness studies tend to use less restrictive inclusion criteria, and include participants with heterogeneous characteristics. They tend to use active controls (e.g. the new anti-hypertensive drug versus a beta-blocker) rather than placebo controls, and flexible regimens (e.g. 20 mg orally every 6 hours, reducing or increasing the dose by 5 mg according to the degree of blood pressure control and adverse effects). They are analyzed to include all of the patients who were allocated to receive the intervention (see Chapter 3). Effectiveness trials often include the use of 'soft' outcome measures, such as measures of sexual function or quality of life.

Both efficacy and effectiveness approaches are reasonable and complementary. They often cannot be clearly differentiated. The terms represent a spectrum and most RCTs include elements from each. The key issue is whether the investigators achieved the best combination of elements to answer their (and the readers') questions.

What is an equivalence trial?

On occasions, trials are designed not to detect possible differences in efficacy or effectiveness between two or more interventions, but to show that the interventions are, within certain narrow limits, 'equally effective' or 'equally efficacious'.[3] These trials are called *equivalence trials*. Often, they seek to demonstrate that a new intervention (or a cheaper or more conservative one) is at least as good as the conventional standard treatment. Investigators who engage in equivalence trials should make efforts to minimize the risk of suggesting that the interventions have equivalent effects when in fact they do not. Strategies to minimize this type of risk are described in Chapters 3 and 4.

What are phase I, II, III, and IV trials?

These terms are used to describe the different types of trials that are conducted during the evaluation of a new drug. Only phase III trials are actually RCTs. Phase I, II, and IV trials are not randomized. They are, however, important stages in the development and understanding of the effects of an intervention.

As the name suggests, *phase I trials* are the first studies conducted in humans to evaluate a new drug. They are conducted once the safety and potential efficacy of the new drug have been documented in animals. As the investigators know nothing about the effects of the new drug in humans, phase I trials tend to focus on *safety*, rather than on comparative effectiveness. They are used to establish how much of a new drug can be given to humans without causing serious adverse effects, and to study how the drug is metabolized by the human body. Phase I trials are mostly conducted on *healthy volunteers*. The typical participant in a phase I study may be one of the investigators who developed the new drug, either an employee of a pharmaceutical company or a member of a research team at a university. People with diseases for which there is no known cure (for instance, certain types of advanced cancer) sometimes participate in phase I trials. As mentioned above, these trials are typically *not randomized*, and even *not controlled*. Usually, they are just series of cases in which the participants are given incremental doses of the drug, without a control group, while they are monitored carefully by the investigators.

After the safety of a new drug has been documented in phase I trials, investigators can proceed to conduct *phase II trials*. These are trials in which the new drug is given to small groups of patients with a given condition. The aim of phase II trials is to establish the relative efficacy of different doses and frequencies of administration. Even though phase II trials focus on efficacy, they can also provide additional information on the safety of the new drug.

Often, phase II trials are not randomized, particularly when the therapeutic effects of the new drug can be measured. For instance, if a new drug has been designed to treat a type of cancer that is associated with a high mortality rate, the investigators will conduct a phase II trial in which about 20 patients will receive the drug while tumor response, mortality, and adverse effects are monitored carefully. If the drug is judged to be ineffective or excessively toxic, no more trials will be conducted. However, if the drug produces a good response (i.e. fewer patients than expected die) and patients tolerate its adverse effects, the investigators can proceed to a phase III trial.

Phase III trials are designed and conducted once a new drug has been shown to be reasonably effective and safe in phase II trials.[4] Phase III trials are typically *effectiveness* trials, because they seek to compare the new drug with an existing drug or intervention known to be effective. This existing drug is usually regarded as the current standard treatment.[4] Most phase III trials are RCTs, the subject of this book.

The term *phase IV* trial is used to represent large studies[3] that seek to monitor adverse effects of a new drug after it has been approved for marketing.[4] These studies are also called post-marketing or post-approval surveillance studies. They are mostly surveys and seldom include comparisons among interventions. Phase IV trials can also be used to bring a new drug to the attention of a large number of clinicians[4] or to expand the number of indications for clinical use.

Physicians and patients both expect that after a drug has been approved for clinical use it will be both safe and effective for the appropriate indications. This expectation may be naïve. Serious adverse effects of drugs may be quite uncommon, and detecting them accurately can be difficult within the context of most RCTs, or with the existing passive, unsystematic, unregulated, uncoordinated, and non-mandatory system for assessing the risk of adverse events of an intervention following its approval by regulatory agencies. Sometimes because of conflicts of interest, pharmaceutical firms or device manufacturers may neglect to promote studies specifically designed to assess the potential harm of their products in the real world, or to fully acknowledge reports that indicate harm. Developers of new and expensive interventions are strongly motivated to protect and expand their markets, and may use highly defensive articles as well as other tactics to do so. Measures to improve post-approval surveillance are at least under consideration, and we hope that they will succeed in penetrating the dense jungle of competing interests.[5]

RCTs according to how the participants are exposed to the interventions

Depending on the way in which the participants are exposed to the study interventions, RCTs can have parallel, factorial, or crossover designs.

What is a parallel design?

Parallel design studies (also called parallel trials or RCTs with parallel group design) are trials in which each group of participants is exposed only to one of the study interventions. They are the most frequently used design. For instance, in a parallel trial designed to compare the effects of a new analgesic with those of a placebo in patients with migraine, the investigators would give the new analgesic to one group of patients and placebo to a *different* group of patients.

What is a factorial design?

In a factorial design, investigators can compare two or more experimental interventions in combination as well as individually. For example, in a factorial design trial to compare the effects of low-dose aspirin and vitamin E in preventing cardiovascular events in patients with diabetes,[6] patients were allocated to receive aspirin only, vitamin E only, both aspirin and vitamin E or placebo. This design allows the investigators to compare the experimental interventions with each other, and with a placebo, and also to investigate interactions between the interventions (i.e. the effects of aspirin and vitamin E given separately with the effects of the combination).

What is a cross-over design?

An RCT has a cross-over design when each of the participants is given *all* the study interventions in successive periods. The order in which the participants receive each of the study interventions is determined at random. Cross-over trials produce *within-participant comparisons*, while parallel designs produce between-participant comparisons. As each participant acts as his/her own control, cross-over can produce statistically significant and clinically important results with fewer participants than would be required with a parallel design.[7,8]

The time during which each of the interventions is administered and evaluated is called a *period*. The simplest cross-over design includes only two periods. Returning to the example of the new analgesic, if the same group of investigators uses a cross-over design, they would randomize *each* patient to receive the new analgesic first and then the placebo, or vice versa, the placebo first and then the new analgesic.

For cross-over trials to be useful, the condition under study must be stable and should not be curable during the first period of the trial (the participants would not be able to receive the control).[9] The effect of the intervention must have a short duration and be reversible. When the effects of one intervention are still present during the evaluation of another, such effects are called *carry-over effects*. If any observed difference between the interventions can be explained by the order in which the interventions were given to the participants, this is called *a treatment–period interaction* and it can invalidate the trial. Carry-over effects can be predicted when the duration of the effects of the interventions are well known. In these cases, carry-over effects can be prevented by separating the study periods by a period of time that is long enough to enable the participants to be free of the influence of the intervention previously used by the time they receive the next intervention.[3] This amount of time is also known as *washout period*.

RCTs according to the unit of analysis

The unit of analysis for an RCT is usually the individual, but sometimes it could be a part of the body (e.g. comparing a treatment used on one limb with a different treatment on the other). On other occasions, the unit has to be larger than the individual.

There are times when randomizing individuals is either technically impossible or may compromise the evaluation. Some interventions can only be delivered to groups. The organization of health care in a community will affect all patients in that community. An intervention aimed at health professions, such as a training package, will (or at least might) modify the care of all patients attended by those professionals. However, randomization in groups has disadvantages in terms of sample size requirement; the number of patients needed will have to be larger because the groups, rather than the individuals will be the unit of analysis. Individuals within each group cannot be considered as independent because, for example, the location of the community or the characteristics of a particular practitioner may attract a particular type of patient. This 'clustering' effect increases the number of subjects required.[10,11]

There may be ethical problems involved with randomization of groups of individuals. Making sure that individual participants are informed of the study may be difficult, and individual patients may not have the opportunity to consent to randomization. This may be acceptable if the potential risk of the intervention is very low, but this would depend on the nature of the intervention (see Chapter 8).

RCTs according to the number of participants

RCTs can have fixed or variable (sequential) numbers of participants. In a fixed-size trial the investigators establish, a priori, the number of participants (the *sample size*) that they will include. This number can be decided arbitrarily or can be calculated using statistical methods. The main goal of using statistical methods to calculate the sample size is to maximize the chance of detecting a statistically and clinically significant difference between the interventions when a difference really exists. In other cases, the investigators do not set the sample size at the outset. Instead, the investigators continue recruiting participants until a clear benefit of one of the interventions is observed, or until they are convinced that there are no important differences between the interventions.[12] These trials allow a more efficient use of resources than trials with fixed numbers of participants, but they depend on the principal outcome being measured relatively soon after trial entry.

How small can a trial be?

Can a trial be done on one person? Surprisingly, perhaps, the answer is yes. These RCTs are called '*n-of-1 trials*' or '*individual patient trials*'. Basically, they are cross-over trials in which one participant receives the experimental and the control interventions in pairs, on multiple occasions, and in random order. Indeed, many researchers consider the n-of-1 trial to be the strongest form of evidence because what we really want to know is whether the treatment will work for *this* person, rather than what its effects are on average. These trials provide results applicable to that individual, rather than generalizable results.

The n-of-1 trials can be very useful when it is not clear whether a treatment will help a particular person. They are particularly applicable for patients with a rare disease when there are no trials supporting the use of the treatment in that particular disease, or for any condition where the treatment has been evaluated in studies that include very different patients.[13] Typically, the number of pairs of interventions varies from 2 to 7. Usually, the number of pairs is not specified in advance, so that the clinician and the patient can decide to stop when they are convinced that there are (or that there are not) important differences between the interventions.

How big can a trial be?

'*Mega-trial*' is a term that is being used to describe RCTs with a simple design which include thousands of patients and limited data collection.[14,15] Usually, these trials require the participation of many investigators (sometimes hundreds of them) from multiple centers and from different countries. The main purpose of these large simple trials is to obtain 'increased statistical power' and to achieve wider generalizability.

RCTs according to whether the investigators and the participants know which intervention is being assessed

In addition to randomization (which helps control selection bias), a randomized trial can incorporate other methodological strategies to reduce the risk of other biases. These biases and the strategies to control them will be discussed in detail in Chapter 3, but we have raised the issue in this chapter because the presence, absence, or degree of one of these strategies have been used to classify RCTs. This strategy is known as *'blinding'* or perhaps more appropriately (but less commonly used) *'masking'*.

In clinical trial jargon, blinding, or masking represents any attempt made by the investigators to keep one or more of the people involved in the trial (e.g. the participant or the person assessing the outcomes) unaware of the intervention that is being given or evaluated. The purpose of blinding is to reduce the risk of *ascertainment or observation bias*. This bias is present when the assessment of the outcomes of an intervention is influenced systematically by knowledge of which intervention a participant is receiving.

The term *'double-blind randomized controlled trial'* is so often used to represent the ultimate in design to produce valid results. This jargon term confuses the issue because the important thing is not the number of people who are blinded (or masked) during a trial, but the number and role of those who are *not* blinded. Anyone of the many people who are involved in a trial can distort its results, if they know the identity of the intervention while it is administered or assessed.

Blinding can be implemented in at least six different levels in an RCT. These levels include the participants, the investigators, or clinicians who administer the interventions, the investigators or clinicians who take care of the participants during the trial, the investigators who assess the outcomes of the interventions, the data analysts and the investigators who write the results of the trial. Of course, in many studies those who administer the interventions, take care of the participants, assess the outcomes, or write the reports are the same. Depending on the extent of blinding, RCTs can be classified as *open* (everyone involved in the trial knows what is happening), or *single-blind, double-blind*, triple-blind, quadruple-blind, and so on.

Successful blinding requires that the interventions be indistinguishable. When the experimental intervention is new and there are no standard effective interventions that could be used as control, the investigators could use an inert substance, or *placebo* that would appear identical to the experimental intervention. These trials are known as *placebo controlled*.

When the RCT is designed to compare a new intervention with a standard treatment, the RCTs are called *active controlled*. Achieving successful blinding in active controlled trials is often difficult and frequently requires the use of what is called a *double-dummy*. In a double-dummy RCT, each group of participants receives one of the active interventions and a placebo (in this case called a dummy) that appears identical to the *other* intervention. The double-dummy technique is particularly useful when the investigators want to compare interventions that are administered by different routes or that require different techniques of administration. For instance, a double-dummy RCT would be the ideal study design to compare one intervention that is given as a tablet with another that is given by injection. In such a trial, the participants in one of the study groups would receive a tablet with the active drug and a placebo injection, while the participants in the other group would receive a placebo tablet and an injection with the active drug.

RCTs that take into account non-randomized individuals and participants' preferences

The preferences of an individual (patient or clinician) for one of the interventions to be compared in a trial could strongly influence the outcome.

If people refuse to participate in a trial because of their preference, the resulting study sample would not be representative of the overall target group. If they participate, despite their preference, they might subvert the protocol either through their compliance or at the time of the assessment of the outcomes. For example, bias may occur when patients who are aware of an experimental treatment not available to them outside a trial decide to join the trial, hoping to receive the treatment, but comply poorly if they receive the control intervention.

The outcomes of the individuals who do not participate in the trials or of those who participate and have strong preferences are rarely recorded. *Preference trials* are designed specifically to overcome this limitation.[16] These trials include at least one group in which the participants are allowed to choose their own preferred treatment from among several options offered.

There are at least three types of preference trials: Zelen's design, trials with a comprehensive cohort design, and Wennberg's design (Figure 2.1).

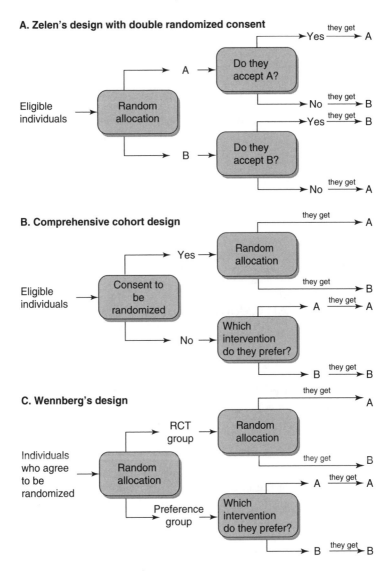

A. Zelen's design with double randomized consent

Eligible individuals → Random allocation
- A → Do they accept A?
  - Yes → they get → A
  - No → they get → B
- B → Do they accept B?
  - Yes → they get → B
  - No → they get → A

B. Comprehensive cohort design

Eligible individuals → Consent to be randomized
- Yes → Random allocation
  - they get → A
  - they get → B
- No → Which intervention do they prefer?
  - A → they get → A
  - B → they get → B

C. Wennberg's design

Individuals who agree to be randomized → Random allocation
- RCT group → Random allocation
  - they get → A
  - they get → B
- Preference group → Which intervention do they prefer?
  - A → they get → A
  - B → they get → B

Figure 2.1 Preference trials

What is a trial with Zelen's design?

In a trial with Zelen's design, eligible individuals are randomized to receive either a standard treatment or an experimental intervention *before they give consent* to participate in the trial. Those who are allocated to standard treatment are given the standard treatment and are not told that they are part of a trial, while those who are allocated to the experimental intervention are offered the experimental intervention and told that they are part of a trial. If they refuse to participate in the trial, they are given the standard intervention but are analyzed as if they had received the experimental intervention.[17]

The main advantages of Zelen's design are that almost all eligible individuals are included in the trial and that the design allows the evaluation of the true effect of *offering* experimental interventions to patients. The main disadvantages are that they have to be open trials and that the statistical power of the study may be affected if a high proportion of participants choose to have the standard treatment.

There are obvious ethical problems in using Zelen's design to randomize patients without their consent, but there may be times when this approach may be kinder to the participants (Chapter 8). To overcome the ethical concerns of not telling patients that they have been randomized to receive the standard treatment, the original approach proposed by Zelen can be modified by informing all participants of the group to which they have been allocated, and by offering them the opportunity to switch to the other group. This design is also known as *double randomized consent design* (Figure 2.1A).

What is a trial with comprehensive cohort design?

A comprehensive cohort trial is a study in which all participants are followed up, regardless of their randomization status (Figure 2.1B). In these trials, if a person agrees to take part in an RCT, she/he is randomized to one of the study interventions. If the person does not agree to be randomized because she/he has a strong preference for one of the interventions that person will be given the preferred intervention and followed up as if she/he was part of a cohort study (Chapter 7).[18,19] At the end, the outcomes of people who participated in the RCT can be compared with those who participated in the cohort studies to assess their similarities and differences.

This type of design is ideal for trials in which a large proportion of eligible individuals are likely to refuse to be randomized because they (or their clinicians) have a strong preference for one of the study interventions.[18] In this case, it could be said that the study is really a prospective cohort study with a small proportion of participants participating in an RCT.

What is a trial with Wennberg's design?

In a trial with Wennberg's design, eligible individuals are randomized to a 'preference group' or to an 'RCT group'[20] (Figure 2.1C). Those individuals in the preference group are given the opportunity to receive the intervention that they choose, while those in the RCT group are allocated randomly to receive any of the study interventions, regardless of their preference. At the end of the study, the outcomes associated with each of the interventions in each of the groups are compared and used to estimate the impact of the participants' preferences on the outcomes.

Preference trials are rarely used in health care research, although they may be more frequently used as consumer participation in health care decisions and research increases.[21] We believe that these study designs are strong, useful, and should be used far more often.

Our musings

With few exceptions, since their introduction into clinical research, trials have followed a simple, basic, and linear recipe: conceive of an intervention that may help cure or alleviate a health problem in a particular population; formulate a question; use chance allocation to divide a sample of the population into two or more groups; use the proposed intervention for one of the groups; and compare the outcomes for that group with the outcomes for the other group or groups who did not receive the intervention. It is a good, robust, recipe that produced a nourishing product. It proved eminently successful for at least half a century.

The recipe is nourishing, but perhaps not delectable. The ingredients are good, but the basic menu may not satisfy the modern palate. Perhaps it is time to look for more varied, more acceptable, and more digestible fare. Recipes that were new and exciting in the middle of the 20th century may not be enough as the new century dawns. Although there have been some innovations in trial design, these have mainly been a tinkering with, rather than a radical look at new possibilities.

In essence, the RCT has followed a linear, cause-and-effect epistemology, an assumption that other things being equal, any differences found between the groups compared will be due to chance, and that they will strictly follow the laws of statistical probability. Sometimes, when problems are fairly simple (such as how to bake a cake, how to treat pneumococcal pneumonia), following a tested recipe will give us a consistently successful product. Sometimes a problem is more complicated (e.g. how to connect a shuttle with a spaceship in orbit, how to anesthetize a patient for chest surgery), but still if the protocol is followed meticulously we can be reasonably confident of a successful result.

Unfortunately, other things are not always equal. Complex issues (e.g. raising a child, how to treat dementia) do not seem to respond to the straightforward cause-and-effect algorithm. We can do all the right things, but our child grows up to be her own self; dementia follows its own inexorable course. How can traditional trials help us? When we try to address important complex issues related to our health and health care with approaches well suited for simple and complicated problems, they are not likely to work. Being more persistent, doing the same thing over and over again, and using more and more resources in the same way, is not likely to produce different results.

It is not hard to understand the popularity of RCTs as currently conceived. They are very convenient for trialists, for pharmaceutical firms, for funding agencies, for regulatory agencies and publishers. They provide clear paths to follow, from the formulation of the research question, through the recruitment of subjects, collection of data, analysis of the results, to the publication of the findings. They satisfy bureaucratic protocols. The question is how good they still are for our health. The problems that concerned us most in the 20th century were primarily acute problems, ones that could be readily identified and delineated, where the responses to treatments could be readily assessed. More and more of our 21st century problems are complex, chronic, difficult to pinpoint, with long-delayed and uncertain responses to our well-meaning interventions.[22]

The very success to date of RCTs for many problems may be blinding us to the opportunities and need for innovative approaches. The mechanistic approach that was right for the industrial age may even be detrimental for an age in which we must acknowledge that uncertainty and unpredictability are unavoidable, and should be cherished. We believe that it is time for radical new designs for RCTs.

Why couldn't we give more prominence to patient preference trials, which recognize the effects that choice may have on outcome?

Why couldn't trials have more democratic designs, in which all who may be affected by the results of a trial are involved in its formulation?

Can we build recursive elements into trials, so that questions be reformulated in response to early findings, or interventions be modified in response to emerging patterns?

Why not investigate qualitative elements concurrently, as integral parts of a randomized trial?

What if we paid more attention to the behavioral aspects of the interventions, and the effects that the trial per se may have on both clinicians and participants?

Is it time to think of the rhetorical aspects of the trial, the effects that they may have on potential users of the information, rather than just the validity of the results?

We know that others will come up with very innovative ideas to further improve RCTs that are more relevant to the needs of today and tomorrow. These ideas may be more difficult to share, they may be resisted, but they may prevail. We hope that they will be given a chance.

It is time for mavericks and academics to leave the assembly line, to recover their role as iconoclasts and innovators. A time to reject bureaucratic mind sets, intolerance of change, and rigid institutional regulations.

References

1. Fletcher RH, Fletcher SW. *Clinical Epidemiology: The Essentials*, 4th edition. Baltimore, MD: Lippincott Williams & Wilkins, 2005.
2. Sackett DL, Gent M. Controversy in counting and attributing events in clinical trials. *New England Journal of Medicine* 1979;301:1410–1412.
3. Armitage P, Berry G, Matthews JNS. *Statistical Methods in Medical Research*, 4th edition. Oxford, UK: Blackwell Publishing Professional, 2001.
4. Pocock SJ. *Clinical Trials: A Practical Approach*. Chichester, UK: John Wiley & Sons, 1983.
5. Fontanarosa PB, Rennie D, DeAngelis CD. Postmarketing surveillance – lack of vigilance, lack of trust. *Journal of American Medical Association* 2004; 292:2647–2650.
6. Sacco M, Pellegrini F, Roncaglioni MC, Avanzini F, Tognoni G, Nicolucci A, PPP Collaborative Group. Primary prevention of cardiovascular events with low-dose aspirin and vitamin E in type 2 diabetic patients: results of the Primary Prevention Project (PPP) trial. *Diabetes Care* 2003; 26: 3264–3272.

7. Louis TA, Lavori PW, Bailar III JC, Polansky M. Crossover and self-controlled designs in clinical research. In *Medical Uses of Statistics*, 2nd edition, JC Bailar III and M Frederick (Eds.). Boston: New England Medical Journal Publications, 1992, pp. 83–104.

8. Sibbald B, Roberts C. Understanding controlled trials: crossover trials. *British Medical Journal* 1998;316:1719–1720.

9. Senn S. *Cross-over Trials in Clinical Research*. Chichester, UK: John Wiley & Sons, 2002.

10. Roberts C, Sibbald B. Understanding controlled trials. Randomising groups of patients. *British Medical Journal* 1998;316:1898–1900.

11. Bland JM, Kerry SM. Trials randomized in clusters. *British Medical Journal* 1997;315:600–660.

12. Altman DG. *Practical Statistics for Medical Research*. London: Chapman & Hall, 1991.

13. Guyatt G, Sackett D, Taylor DW, Chong J, Roberts RS, Pugsley S. Determining optimal therapy – randomized trials in individual patients. *New England Journal of Medicine* 1986;314:889–892.

14. Woods KL. Mega-trials and management of acute myocardial infarction. *Lancet* 1995;346:611–614.

15. Charlton BG. Mega-trials: methodological issues and clinical implications. *Journal of the Royal College of Physicians of London* 1995;29:96–100.

16. King et al. Impact of participant and physician intervention preferences on randomized trials: a systematic review. *Journal of American Medical Association* 2005;293:1089–1099.

17. Zelen M. A new design for randomized clinical trials. *New England Journal of Medicine* 1979;300:1242–1245.

18. Olschewski M, Scheurlen H. Comprehensive cohort study: an alternative to randomized consent design in a breast preservation trial. *Methods of Information in Medicine* 1985;24:131–134.

19. Brewin CR, Bradley C. Patient preferences and randomised clinical trials. *British Medical Journal* 1989;299:684–685.

20. Flood AB, Wennberg JE, Nease Jr RF, Fowler Jr FJ, Ding J, Hynes LM. The importance of patient preference in the decision to screen for prostate cancer. *Journal of General Internal Medicine* 1996;11:342–349.

21. Sackett DL, Wennberg JE. Choosing the best research design for each question. *British Medical Journal* 1997;315:1636.

22. www.healthandeverything.org (accessed December 22, 2006).

CHAPTER 3

Bias in randomized controlled trials

The main appeal of the randomized controlled trial (RCT) in health care comes from its potential to reduce selection bias. Randomization, if done properly, can keep study groups as similar as possible at the outset, so that the investigators can isolate and quantify the effect of the interventions they are studying. No other study design gives us the power to balance unknown prognostic factors at baseline. Random allocation does not, however, protect RCTs against other types of bias.

The existence of most biases related to RCTs is supported mainly by common sense. In recent years, however, important research efforts have used RCTs as the subject rather than the tool of research. These studies are usually designed to generate empirical evidence to improve the design, reporting, dissemination, and use of RCTs in health care.[1] They have confirmed that RCTs are vulnerable to many types of bias throughout their entire life span. Random allocation of the participants to different study groups increases the potential of a study to be free of allocation bias, but has no effect on other important biases.

In this chapter we will discuss the concept of bias in relation to RCTs and highlight some of its sources. We will also list a variety of biases, as well as some strategies that may help us recognize them and minimize their impact on the planning of research and health-related decisions.

What is bias?

An online dictionary[2] defines 'bias' as '*a partiality that prevents objective consideration of an issue or situation*'. In statistics it means '*a tendency of an estimate to deviate in one direction from a true value.*[3] This systematic deviation from the true value can result in either underestimation or overestimation of the effects of an intervention. Because there is usually more interest in showing that a new intervention works than in showing that it does not work, biases in clinical trials most often lead to an exaggeration in the magnitude or importance of the effects of new interventions.

We should not jump to the conclusion that bias in health research is necessarily associated with a conscious or malicious attempt of investigators, funders, or readers to bend the results of a trial. Indeed, although bias may be introduced into a trial intentionally, it is probably more commonly unintentional, and often unrecognized even by the researchers themselves.

Why does bias in an RCT matter?

The true effects of any health care intervention are unknown. We try to anticipate, detect, quantify, and control bias to produce results from a sample of participants that can be generalized to the target population at large. It is impossible to ever know for sure whether the results of a particular study are biased, simply because it is impossible to establish whether those results depart systematically from a 'truth' that remains unknown.

What are the main types of bias in RCTs?

Most discussions on bias focus on biases that can occur during the actual course of a trial, from the allocation of participants to study groups, through the delivery of interventions, to the measurement of outcomes. Other types of bias can arise, however, even before the trial is carried out, in the choice of problem to study or type of research to use, or after the trial is carried out, in its analysis, and its dissemination. Bias can even be introduced by the person who is reading the report of a trial.[4] These biases, which can also have a profound influence on the way in which the results of RCTs are interpreted and used, tend to receive less attention.

To illustrate how biases can affect the results of an RCT, we invite you to think about the following hypothetical scenario:

'Imagine a new drug for the treatment of multiple sclerosis, which has shown promising results in animal studies and in phase I trials. These results, which suggest that the drug can delay the onset of severe motor

compromise, have been widely publicized by the media during the past 3 months. Because of these results, patient advocacy groups are putting pressure on the government to make the new drug available as soon as possible. As multiple sclerosis is a debilitating disease that affects millions of people worldwide and for which there is no known cure, the investigators (all clinicians who have dealt with multiple sclerosis patients for years), the company producing the new drug (which has invested millions in developing the drug), the media (interested in confirming the results that they so widely publicized) and the potential participants (patients with multiple sclerosis who have been waiting for an effective treatment to be discovered) are all interested in demonstrating that the new compound is effective. After many intense sessions debating the course of action, a multidisciplinary task force created by the government, including consumer representatives, agrees that the next step should be a randomized clinical trial. A research protocol is produced by another multidisciplinary panel of investigators and consumers, and a well known research group at a large health care center is selected to conduct the study.'

We discuss the elements of this hypothetical scenario in the following sections.

Selection bias

With true randomization, all participants in the study are given the same opportunity to be allocated or assigned to each of the study groups. But even a perfectly randomized method to allocate participants to the study groups does not protect against selection bias, which can occur both in the way that individuals are accepted or rejected for participation in a trial, and in the way that the interventions are assigned to individuals once they have been accepted into a trial.

Selection bias can occur if some potentially eligible individuals are selectively excluded from the study, because the investigator knows the group to which they would be allocated if they participated. Let us suppose that the investigator in charge of recruiting patients for the multiple sclerosis trial (who at least subconsciously hopes that the drug will be found to be effective) thinks that depressed patients are less likely to respond to the new drug. If he has access to the allocation sequence (which has been generated by computer and is locked in his desk) this investigator could introduce bias into the trial by making it more difficult for depressive patients to receive the new drug. He could, knowingly or unknowingly, exclude depressive patients who would be allocated to receive the new drug by making them fit the exclusion criteria more easily than if they had been allocated to the placebo group. He could also (again knowingly or unknowingly) present information on the trial to depressive patients allocated to receive the new drug in such a way that they would be discouraged from consenting to participate. At the end of the trial, if the investigator was right, and depressive patients were in truth less likely to respond to the new drug, the trial will show an exaggerated effect of the new drug during the treatment of multiple sclerosis, due to the disproportionate number of depressive patients in the placebo group.

How can selection bias be reduced?

There is empirical evidence to show that effects of new interventions can be exaggerated if the randomization sequence is not concealed from the investigators at the time of obtaining consent from prospective trial participants.[5] One study showed that trials with inadequate allocation concealment can exaggerate the estimate of the effect size of interventions by as much as 40% on average.[6] The irony is that *allocation concealment* is a very simple maneuver that can be incorporated in the design of any trial and that can always be implemented.

Despite its simplicity as a maneuver and its importance to reduce bias, allocation concealment is rarely reported, and perhaps rarely implemented in RCTs. Allocation concealment was reported in less than 10% of articles describing RCTs published in prominent journals in five different languages.[7] This does not necessarily mean that allocation is not concealed in 90% of RCTs; in some cases, allocation may have been concealed, but the authors, peer-reviewers, and journal editors were not aware of how important it is to mention it (it takes about a line in the report, so space limitation is not a good excuse). If, however, allocation concealment was not carried out in most cases in which it was not reported, the majority of RCTs are at risk of exaggerating the effects of the interventions they were designed to evaluate.

Even if the report of an RCT states that efforts were made to conceal the allocation sequence, there are many ways in which randomization can be subverted by investigators who want to break the allocation code before they obtain consent from prospective trial participants.[8] Even when the allocation codes are kept in sealed opaque envelopes, for instance, investigators can (and sometimes do) look through the envelopes using powerful lights or even open the envelope using steam and reseal it without others noticing. Thus it is very easy to introduce selection bias into RCTs.

Users of RCTs should not get a false sense of security just because a study is randomized.

Ascertainment bias

Ascertainment bias occurs when the results or conclusions of a trial are systematically distorted by knowledge of which intervention each participant is receiving. Ascertainment bias can be introduced by the person administering the interventions, the person receiving the interventions (the participants), the investigator assessing or analyzing the outcomes, and even by the people who write the report describing the trial (Chapter 2).

The best way to protect a trial against ascertainment bias is by keeping the people involved in the trial unaware of the identity of the interventions for as long as possible. This is called blinding or masking. The strategies that can be used to reduce ascertainment bias can be applied during at least two periods of a trial: the time during which data are collected actively (from the administration of the interventions to the gathering of outcome data) and after data have been collected (from data analysis to the reporting of results).

It is important to recognize the difference between biases that are the result of lack of allocation concealment and biases that arise from lack of blinding. *Allocation concealment* helps to prevent selection bias, protects the randomization sequence *before* and *until* the interventions are given to study participants, and can *always* be implemented. *Blinding* helps prevent ascertainment bias, protects the randomization sequence *after* allocation, and cannot always be implemented.[6]

How can ascertainment bias be reduced during data collection?

Ascertainment bias can be introduced in different ways during data collection. For instance, the people administering the interventions can bias the results of a trial by altering systematically the co-interventions given to participants during the trial. Following our example of the multiple sclerosis trial, the new drug may appear to be more effective at the end of the trial if patients allocated to the new drug received physiotherapy earlier and more intensively than patients allocated to placebo (*co-intervention bias*). If participants know that they have been allocated to the placebo group, they are likely to feel disappointed and less willing to report improvement at each of the study time points (*participant ascertainment bias*). In addition, if the people in charge of assessing and recording the outcomes know which patients are allocated to each of the study groups, they could, consciously or unconsciously, tend to record the outcomes for patients receiving the new drug in a more favorable way than for patients receiving placebo (*observer bias*).

In ideal circumstances, ascertainment bias should be reduced by blinding all concerned: the individuals who administer the interventions, the participants who receive the interventions and the individuals in charge of assessing and recording the outcomes (Chapter 2).

The importance of blinding has been confirmed in empirical studies. It has been shown, for instance, that open studies are more likely to favor experimental interventions over the controls[9] and that studies that are not double-blinded can exaggerate effect estimates by 17%.[6] Despite the empirical evidence available, and common sense, only about half of the trials that could be double-blinded actually were.[10] Even when the trials are described as double-blind, most reports do not provide adequate information on how blinding was achieved or statements on the perceived success (or failure) of double-blinding efforts.[11,12]

The best strategy to achieve blinding during data collection is with the use of placebos. *Placebos* are interventions believed to be inactive, but otherwise identical to the experimental intervention in all aspects other than the postulated specific effect. Placebos are certainly easier to develop and implement successfully in drug trials, in which they should resemble the taste, smell and appearance of the active drug, and should be given using an identical procedure.

Placebo controls can also be used with non-drug interventions, such as psychological, physical, and surgical procedures, although they are more difficult to develop and implement successfully. For example, it is difficult, but not impossible to develop and implement placebo counseling, physiotherapy, acupuncture or electrical stimulation. In some cases it is impossible, unfeasible or simply unethical to use placebos. It would be impossible, for example, to use a placebo intervention in a trial evaluating the effect on mothers and newborns of early versus late discharge from hospital after childbirth. It would be unfeasible or unethical to use a placebo in trials evaluating new or existing surgical interventions (although a strong case can still be made for trials in which sham surgery can successfully challenge the perceived effectiveness of surgical interventions).[13] Placebo controlled studies are not ethical to study a new or existing intervention when there is an effective intervention available (Chapter 8). Even in cases where the use of placebos is impossible, unfeasible or unethical, trials can be at least single blind. In a surgical or acupuncture trial, for instance, single-blinding can be achieved by keeping the investigators in charge of assessing the outcomes unaware of which participants receive which interventions.

How can ascertainment bias be reduced after data collection?

Ascertainment bias can be introduced easily after data collection, if the investigators in charge of analyzing or reporting the results of the trial are aware of which participants are receiving which interventions. The effects of a new intervention can be exaggerated, for instance, if the investigators in charge of analyzing the trial data select the outcomes and the time points that show maximum benefit from the new intervention and ignore outcomes and time points that show either no effect or harm from the new intervention. Similarly, investigators in charge of reporting the trial results can choose to emphasize the outcomes and time points that show the maximum effects of the new intervention, downplaying or ignoring findings that suggest that the new intervention is equivalent or less effective than the control.

This source of bias can be controlled by keeping the data analysts and the people in charge of reporting the trial results unaware of the identity of the study groups. In a study with two groups, for instance, the outcome data could be given to analysts coded as A and B, and once they complete the analysis, the results could be given to the person in charge of writing the report using the same codes. The codes would not be broken until after the data analysis and reporting phases were completed. These valuable strategies should be used and studied more often.

Other important sources of bias

What biases can occur during the planning phase of an RCT?

Choice-of-question bias

Perhaps one of the least recognized forms of bias in an RCT is hidden in the choice of the question that the trial intends to answer. This would not necessarily affect the internal validity of a trial, but may have profound effects on its external validity, or generalizability. This bias can take many forms.

Hidden agenda bias occurs when a trial is mounted, not in order to answer a question, but in order to demonstrate a pre-required answer. The unspoken converse may be 'Don't do a trial if it won't show you what you want to find'. This could be called the *vested interest bias*.[14] Closely related to this is the *self fulfiling prophecy bias*, in which the very carrying out of a trial ensures the desired result.

The *cost and convenience bias* can seriously compromise what we choose to study. When we study what we can afford to study, or what is convenient to study, rather than what we really want to study, or should study, we take resources away from what we know is important. Closely related to this is the *funding availability bias* where studies tend to concentrate on questions that are more readily fundable, often for a vested or commercial interest. We should always look for the *secondary gains search bias* which can influence the choice of study, the methodology used, and the ascertainment and dissemination of the results.

Regulation bias

This is sometimes referred to as the *IRB bias* or the *Bureaucracy bias*. It occurs when institutional review boards are overly restrictive, and block the study of important questions. It also occurs when they are overly permissive and allow or even encourage studies that may not be scientifically or socially valid, but may bring either funding or prestige to the institution. Complicated 'informed consent' regulations may block the participation of many otherwise eligible subjects, and hence bias the results (Chapter 8).

Wrong design bias

The perceived value of an RCT may sometimes induce researchers to use this design for questions that may be better (or can only be answered) with a different design, such as outcome research.[15] The wrong research design can produce misleading answers.

What biases can occur during the course of an RCT?

Population choice bias

The sample population studied can have a major effect on the generalizability of an RCT. If the sample is overly restricted by not including women (*gender bias*) or people over (or under) a specific age group (*age bias*), the results may not be generalizable to people who do not belong to the groups. *Pregnancy bias,* (excluding pregnant women) may sometimes be necessary for reasons of safety to the fetus, but the exclusion must be carefully noted. The same reasoning is required when trials are restricted to, or exclude, people in special circumstances (*special circumstances bias*).

Population choice may be restricted when potential participants are approached (*recruitment bias*) or during registration of participants. Eligible patients may be kept out of a trial because they do not understand the consent form (*informed consent bias, literacy bias, language bias*).

Severity of illness bias is an important subgroup of the sample choice bias. Patients with a mild form of an illness may not respond in the same way as those with a more severe form.

Intervention choice bias

The nature of the intervention chosen can have a major effect on the results obtained. The stage at which an intervention is studied can be very important. The *too early bias* and the *too late bias* can determine the effects found.[16] This holds particularly true for surgical trials where there can be a *learning curve bias* for new operators, or improvements (or regression) in the techniques or contexts in which they are used. Similar concerns may hold for medical interventions, when dose or timing of a medication may be important determinants of the outcome.

Complexity bias can occur when a trial is used to study complex interventions, with a number of components, or where outcomes may depend on multiple contingencies outside of the control of the investigator (e.g. the skill of the surgeons or the resources of the community).[17]

Comparison choice (or control group) bias

If an intervention is compared to a poorly chosen control group, it can erroneously appear to be more (or less) effective than it really is. If a study compares an experimental intervention with a placebo control, the results will only tell us whether the intervention has a specific effect or not. It will not imply that the experimental intervention has a different or better effect than existing alternatives. An obvious way to make an intervention appear to be more effective than it really is would be to choose an ineffective comparison group.

Unfortunately, current regulatory bodies that mandate placebo controls lead to carrying out studies with this limited clinical value.

Outcome choice bias

Sometimes RCTs evaluate outcomes that are easy to measure, rather than the outcomes that are relevant (*measurement bias*). One variant of this is the *time term bias* in which short-term outcomes are measured rather than the important long-term outcomes. It is not surprising that researchers sometimes yield to the temptation to study outcomes that are readily measured rather than those that are important.

What biases can occur during the reporting of a trial?

Withdrawal bias: bias introduced by inappropriate handling of withdrawals, drop outs, and protocol violations

Ideally, all participants in a trial should complete the study, follow the protocol, and provide data on all the outcomes of interest at all time points. In reality, however, most trials have missing data. Data can be missing because some of the participants drop out before the end of the trial, because participants do not follow the protocol either deliberately or accidentally, or because some outcomes are not measured correctly or cannot be measured at all at one or more time points.

Regardless of the cause, inappropriate handling of the missing information can lead to bias. For instance, if in the multiple sclerosis trial patients who do not obtain benefit from the new drug withdraw more frequently because of adverse effects, their exclusion from analysis would lead the investigators to exaggerate the benefit and underestimate the harm of the new drug. This bias can occur independently of whether or not the investigators are aware of the identity of the interventions received by the participants. If the decisions on withdrawals have been made because of knowledge of the interventions received by the participants, this constitutes yet another cause of ascertainment bias.

On occasion, it is impossible to know the status of participants at the times when the missing information should have been collected. This could happen, for example, if participants move to different areas during the study or fail to contact the investigators for an unknown reason. If the reasons for excluding these participants or specific outcome measurements from the final analysis were in any way related to the intervention, this could also lead to bias.

There are two strategies that can confidently be assumed to eliminate bias in these circumstances. One is known as *intention-to-treat analysis*, which means that all the study participants are included in the analyses as part of the groups to which they were randomized, regardless of whether they completed the study or not. The second method is a *worst-case scenario* or *sensitivity analysis*. This is performed by assigning the worst possible outcomes to the missing patients or time points in the group that shows the best results, and the best possible outcomes to the missing patients or timepoints in the group with the worst results. We can then see whether the new analysis contradicts or supports the results of the initial analysis excluding the missing data.

Selective reporting bias

A major and common source of bias in an RCT is selective reporting of results, describing those outcomes with positive results, or which favor the studied intervention. This is not always consciously done. The investigator may even unconsciously be attracted more to certain outcomes than others. Variants of this have been named the *social desirability bias* in which the items that are desired, or the *optimism bias* in which the items hoped for, are more likely to be reported.

The *data dredging bias* is another variant of the selective reporting bias. Having looked at all the data, the investigators can report the outcomes they wish to stress, and not mention the less desirable outcomes. A variant is the *interesting data bias*, in which the authors report the data that they find most interesting. The acme of data dredging can be in the selective analysis of data. If unethically contrived, all trials can be made to appear to have positive results.[18]

Fraud bias
Intentional fraud is perhaps the most important, most serious, and most difficult to detect source of bias. We hope that it is rare, but the extent to which fraudulent results are reported may be under-estimated, and may be increasing under the pressure to produce results, no matter how.

What biases can occur during the dissemination of the trials?

What is publication bias?
Investigators and sponsors are more likely to write and submit, and peer-reviewers and editors to accept, manuscripts with positive results for publication. This tendency has been called *publication bias*.[19,20] A systematic review of five empirical methodological studies published mostly during the previous 10 years confirmed that the failure to publish is not a random event, but is heavily influenced by the direction and strength of research findings, whereby manuscripts with statistically significant (positive) results are published preferentially over manuscripts reporting nonsignificant (negative) results.[21] Publication bias may be the main factor behind the systematic differences found between studies funded by industry and their counterparts.[14,22]

Efforts have been made to eliminate publication bias through compulsory registration of trials at inception, and publication of the results of all trials. These have been the focus of intense debate and controversy for several years, fueled by strong ethical and economic interests. Many major journals now refuse to publish the results of studies that had not been registered at inception. Even so, readers must be aware that by relying on published studies to guide their decisions they are always at risk of overestimating the effect of interventions[23–25] (see Chapter 5).

What is language bias?
Recently, a variation of publication bias has been described as *language bias*, to indicate that manuscripts may be submitted to and published by journals in different languages depending on the direction of their results. More studies with positive results may be published in English.[26] A variant of this is the *country of publication bias*, the tendency by some countries to publish a disproportionate number of positive trials.[27]

What is time lag bias?

This bias occurs when the speed of publication depends on the direction and strength of the trial results. In general, it seems that trials with 'negative' results take twice as long to be published as 'positive' trials.[28,29]

What biases can occur during the uptake phase?

Up to this point we have focused on the biases introduced by the investigators who plan and carry out randomized trials, or those who publish and disseminate the results. As this book is primarily a user's guide, rather than a manual for researchers, we felt that we should emphasize the responsibility of the reader of research studies.

Different types of reader biases were described many years ago.[4] At the time in which they were reported, the existence of these biases was supported only by common sense and experience. Recently, there have been empirical studies that support the existence of reader bias, showing that there are systematic differences in the way readers assess the quality of RCTs depending on whether the assessments are conducted under masked or open conditions.[11,30] These studies, however, do not focus on any specific type of reader bias.

The following are some of the biases that we believe are most common and pertinent:

Relation to the author bias, with its subgroups *Rivalry bias* (underrating the strengths or exaggerating the weaknesses of studies published by a rival) and *I owe him one* bias (favoring flawed results from a study by someone who did the same for the reader).

Personal habit bias occurs when readers overrate or underrate a study depending on their own habits (e.g. a reader who enjoys eating animal fat overrating a study that challenges the adverse effects of animal fat on health). This is similar to the *moral bias*, in which readers overrate or underrate a study depending on how much it agrees or disagrees with their moral views (e.g. a reader who regards abortion as immoral overrating a study showing a relationship between abortion and breast cancer). This is closely related to the *values bias* (depending on how important you consider the outcomes of the study to be).

Clinical practice bias takes place when readers judge a study according to whether it supports or challenges their current or past clinical practice (e.g. a clinician who gives lidocaine to patients with acute myocardial infarction underrating a study that suggests that lidocaine may increase mortality in these patients). This is similar to the *institution bias* (that is, or is not, the way that we do it in our hospital), and the *territory bias* which can occur when readers over-rate studies that support their own specialty or profession (e.g. a surgeon favoring a study that suggests that surgery is more effective than medical treatment, or obstetricians underrating a study that suggests that midwives can provide adequate care during uncomplicated pregnancies and deliveries). *Tradition bias* happens when a reader rates a study depending on whether it supports or challenges traditional procedures (e.g. underrating a study that challenges episiotomy during normal vaginal deliveries).

Do something bias means overrating a study that suggests that an intervention is effective, particularly when there is no alternative effective intervention available. This bias may be common among clinicians and patients (e.g. a patient with AIDS overrating a study describing a cure for AIDS).

In this general heading we can include the *technology bias*, which relates to judging a study according to the reader's attraction or aversion for technology in health care. *Resource allocation bias* happens when readers have a strong preference for one type of resource allocation. This bias may be one of the most frequently found in health care, as it can emanate from consumers, clinicians, policy makers, researchers, and fund holders.

Printed word bias occurs when a study is overrated because of undue confidence in published data. Subgroups of the printed word bias include the *prestigious journal bias* (the results of studies published in prestigious journals are overrated), and its opposite, the *non-prestigious journal bias*. Similar to this is the *peer review bias*, which comes into play when readers have an unwarranted belief in the ability of peer review to guarantee the validity of a study.

Prominent author bias occurs when the results of studies published by prominent authors are overrated, and, of course has its converse in the *unknown or non-prominent author bias*. This has been called the '*who is s/he? bias*'.[4] Similar to these are the *famous institution bias*, the *credential or professional background bias* (e.g. physicians underrating research done by nurses or vice versa; basic scientists underrating research done by clinicians or vice versa; PhDs underrating studies published by MDs and vice versa; readers overrating research by authors with many letters after their names and vice versa). Their variants include the *esteemed author bias, esteemed professor bias*, and the *friendship bias*; when the reader overrates results obtained by a close friend or mentor.

We are not through yet!

Geography bias occurs when studies are judged according to the country or region where it was conducted, and is closely related to the *language bias* (e.g. the belief that studies published in languages other than English are of inferior quality than those published in English).[26]

The *trial design bias* can go in either direction. The *favored design bias* occurs when a study that uses a design supported, publicly or privately, by the reader (e.g. a consumer advocate overrating an RCT that takes into account patient preferences). Its converse is the *Disfavored design bias*. Somewhat related are the *large trial bias*, in which the results of large trials are overrated, and the *multicentre trial bias* when the results of multicentre collaborative trials are overrated. The *small trial bias* occurs when the results of trials with small sample size are underrated, particularly when they contradict the opinion of the reader (i.e. attributing to chance any statistically or clinically significant effect found by a small trial, or any lack of significant effects to low power).

Complementary medicine bias refers to the systematic overrating or underrating of studies that describe complementary medicine interventions, particularly when the results suggest that the interventions are effective.

Flashy title bias occurs when the results of studies with attractive titles are overrated (particularly by patients or journalists) or underrated (particularly by academics if they regard them as sensationalist!). Other rather tricky biases include the *substituted question bias,* when a reader substitutes a question for the question that the study is designed to answer and regards the results of the study as invalid if they do not answer the substituted question.

Vested interest bias has a number of subgroups. *Bankbook bias* occurs when a study is rated depending on the impact of its results on the income of the reader (e.g. a surgeon underrating a study that questions the need for surgery to relieve back pain in patients with spinal stenosis, or a pharmaceutical company overrating the results of a study that supports the use of one of its products). *Cherished belief bias* reminds us that there are other competing interests besides the financial ones.

Reader attitude biases include the *Belligerence bias* which results in underrating studies systematically just for the sake of being difficult; the *Empiricism bias* (overrating or underrating a study because it challenges the clinical experience of the reader), or the *I am an epidemiologist bias* in which the reader repudiates a study that contains any flaw, albeit minor, in its design, analysis or interpretation.

Finally, *careless reading bias* occurs when a study is overrated or underrated because the reader neglected to read a key section. Unfortunately, far too common.

Musings

This has been a difficult chapter to write. We approached it with fear and trepidation, feeling part of a 'no win' situation. We know that the control of bias is the *raison d'etre* for clinical trials, and accept that control of bias is the most important factor in diminishing inevitable error. We know that allocation bias is a major source of potential error in clinical comparison studies, and we know that randomization, if properly done, can control for allocation bias. We want to stress the value of randomization for this purpose, and the vital importance of RCTs.

But we also realize that randomization *per se* can control *only* for allocation bias, and this does not even completely control for selection bias. Other biases can also subvert the validity of conclusions at any stage in the planning, conduct, analysis, or interpretation of the results. As we worked together on this chapter, as we uncovered an increasing number of biases, our fears mounted. We started to feel very discouraged. What is the big deal, if this seemingly powerful tool is so vulnerable? Why should we believe in trials if they can be subverted so easily and at so many levels? If biases cannot be controlled, what is left? We are not sufficiently naïve to think that by finding biases and naming them that we can overcome them. Can we run the risk that by drawing attention to the biases we would attack the very foundation of RCTs, and appear to advocate nihilism?

We believed (and still believe) in the value of RCTs. We felt like heretics, not for the first time.[31] Both of us were, and are, strong and enthusiastic proponents of RCTs. Indeed our support for RCTs has become even stronger as we have become more aware of their limitations. But it is no longer a blind faith, rather one that has been through and survived the crises of doubt.

We are concerned with the danger that RCTs may be perceived as a sort of talisman, to protect us from the evil of bias. But randomized trials are not divine revelations, they are human constructs, and like all human constructs, are fallible. They are valuable, useful tools that should be used wisely and well. We believe that a strong belief in the strength of randomized trials, without acknowledging their weaknesses, runs the risk of fundamentalism and intolerance of criticism, or alternative views. In this way, it can discourage innovation.

Our list of biases is far from exhaustive. The number of possible biases is practically infinite, as is the names that can be given to them, or the ways in which they can be classified or categorized. RCTs can never be completely objective. They should be carried out with humility; the investigator should be as up front, explicit, and transparent as possible about his or her motivations for choosing to carry out the trial, the methods used, the outcomes looked for as well as the outcomes found. Journalists have an important responsibility to assume, because of their influence on public understanding. At present they tend to bring to public attention the results of trials purporting beneficial effects of a new intervention for incurable diseases, while they ignore the results of previous (or concurrent) trials in which the same intervention showed no benefit.[32] This media coverage may influence the decisions of clinicians and patients who are not aware of the other studies. The same onus must be put on the reader, the one who will be making use of the information gleaned from the trial. It can be far too easy to criticize an RCT, or to read into it what we want, to find rather than what the results actually show.

Our bottom line is that a new sense of freedom can emerge, as we free ourselves from a false sense of objectivity, and can recognize and use RCTs as the valuable tools that they are, when they are the right tool in the right place.

References

1. Jadad AR, Rennie D. The randomized controlled trial gets a middle-aged checkup. *Journal of American Medical Association* 1998;279:319–320.
2. http://www.wordreference.com/definition/bias (accessed December 22, 2006).
3. *Webster's Third New International Dictionary*, Unabridged. G&C Merriam Co, 1976.
4. Owen R. Reader bias. *Journal of American Medical Association* 1982; 247:2533–2534.
5. Chalmers TC, Celano P, Sacks HS, Smith H. Bias in treatment assignment in controlled clinical trials. *New England Journal of Medicine* 1983; 309:1359–1361.

6. Schulz KF, Chalmers I, Hayes RJ, Altman DG. Empirical evidence of bias: dimensions of methodological quality associated with estimates of treatment effects in controlled trials. *Journal of American Medical Association* 1995;273:408–412.

7. Moher D, Fortin P, Jadad AR, Juni P, Klassen T, Le Lorier J, Liberati A, Linde K, Penna A. Completeness of reporting of trials published in languages other than English: implications for conduct and reporting of systematic reviews. *Lancet* 1996;347:363–366.

8. Schulz KF. Subverting randomization in controlled trials. *Journal of American Medical Association* 1995;274:1456–1458.

9. Colditz GA, Miller JN, Mosteller F. How study design affects outcomes in comparisons of therapy. I: Therapy. *Statistics in Medicine* 1989;8:441–454.

10. Schulz KF, Grimes DA, Altman DG, Hayes RJ. Blinding and exclusions after allocation in randomised controlled trials: survey of published parallel group trials in obstetrics and gynaecology. *British Medical Journal* 1996;312:742–744.

11. Jadad AR, Moore RA, Carroll D, Jenkinson C, Reynolds JM, Gavaghan DJ, McQuay DM. Assessing the quality of reports on randomized clinical trials: Is blinding necessary? *Controlled Clinical Trials* 1996;17:1–12.

12. Moher D, Jadad AR, Tugwell P. Assessing the quality of randomized controlled trials. *International Journal of Technology Assessment in Health Care* 1996;12:195–208.

13. Freeman TB. Use of placebo surgery in controlled trials of a cellular-based therapy for Parkinson's disease. *New England Journal of Medicine* 1999;34:988–992.

14. Fries JF, Krishnan E. Equipoise, design bias, and randomized controlled trials: the elusive ethics of new drug development. *Arthritis Research and Therapy* 2004;6:R250–R255.

15. Sackett DL, Wennberg JE. Choosing the best research design for each question: It's time to stop squabbling over the 'best' methods. *British Medical Journal* 1997;315:1636.

16. Lilford RJ, Braunholtz DA, Greenhalgh R, Edwards SJL. Trials and fast changing technologies: the case for tracker studies. *British Medical Journal* 2000;320;43–46.

17. Kotaska A. Inappropriate use of randomised trials to evaluate complex phenomena: case study of vaginal breech delivery. *British Medical Journal* 2004;329:1039–1042

18. Martin G. Munchausen's statistical grid, which makes all trials significant. *Lancet* 1984;ii:1457.

19. Dickersin K. The existence of publication bias and risk factors for its occurrence. *Journal of American Medical Association* 1990;263: 1385–1389.

20. Rennie D, Flanagin A. Publication bias – the triumph of hope over experience. *Journal of American Medical Association* 1992;267:411–412.

21. Dickersin K. How important is publication bias? A synthesis of available data. *AIDS Education Prevention* 1997;9(Suppl A):15–21.

22. Smith R. Medical Journals are an extension of the marketing arm of pharmaceutical companies. http://medicine.plosjournals.org/perlserv/?request=get-document&doi=10.1371/journal.pmed.0020124 (accessed November 21, 2006)

23. Begg C, Cho M, Eastwood S, Horton R, Moher D, Olkin I, Pitkin R, Rennie D, Schulz KF, Simel D, Stroup DF. Improving the quality of reporting of randomized controlled trials. The CONSORT statement. *Journal of American Medical Association* 1996;276:637–639.

24. Grimes DA. The 'CONSORT' guidelines for randomized controlled trials in Obstetrics and Gynecology. *Obstetrics and Gynecology* 2002;100:631–632.

25. Rennie D. How to report randomized controlled trials. The CONSORT statement. *Journal of American Medical Association* 1996;276:649.

26. Moher D, Pham B, Lawson ML, Klassen TP. The inclusion of reports of randomised trials published in languages other than English in systematic reviews. *Health Technology Assessment* 2003;7:1–90.

27. Vickers A, Goyal N, Harland R, Rees R. Do certain countries produce only positive results? A systematic review of controlled trials. *Controlled Clinical Trials* 1998;19:159–166.

28. Ioannidis JPA. Effect of the statistical significance of results on the time to completion and publication of randomized efficacy trials: a survival analysis. *Journal of American Medical Association* 1998;279:281–286.

29. Stern JM, Simes RJ. Publication bias: evidence of delayed publication in a cohort study of clinical research projects. *British Medical Journal* 1997;315:640–645.

30. McNutt RA, Evans AT, Fletcher RH, Fletcher SW. The effects of blinding on the quality of peer review. A randomized trial. *Journal of American Medical Association* 1990;263:1371–1376.

31. Enkin MW, Jadad AR. Using anecdotal information in evidence-based health care: heresy or necessity? *Annals of Oncology* 1998;9:963–966.

32. Koren G, Klein N. Bias against negative studies in newspaper reports of medical research. *Journal of American Medical Association* 1991;266:1824–1826.

CHAPTER 4

Assessing the quality of randomized controlled trials: why, what, how, and by whom?

If all trials were perfect, we would not have to worry about their quality. Instead, we could always use them with confidence, as part of our decision-making process. To be perfect, among other things, trials would be designed in a way that would balance out all possible competing interests, and help to answer clear, relevant, previously unanswered questions. They would be conducted, and reported by researchers who did not have conflicts of interest, and who follow strict ethical principles.

They would have to evaluate all possible interventions, for all possible variations of the conditions of interest, in all possible types of patients, in all settings, using all relevant outcome measures. Moreover, they would include all available patients, and make full use of strategies to eliminate bias during the administration of the interventions, the evaluation of the outcomes, and reporting of the results, thus reflecting the true effect of the interventions.

The data would be properly analyzed statistically, and would include individual patient data, and an accurate description of the patients who were included, excluded, withdrawn, and who dropped out. The reports, which would give an exact account of all the events that occurred during the design and course of the trial, would be written in clear and unambiguous language.

Unfortunately, a perfect trial can only exist in our imagination. In real life, researchers can only do the best that they can, and report it as clearly as they can. Readers only have imperfect trial reports to read, and face major barriers as they try to determine their quality.

What do we mean by trial quality?

Like beauty, quality must be in the eye of the beholder. It can mean different things to different people, at different times, with different needs. Trial quality is a complex concept, or *construct*. As with most constructs, such as anxiety, happiness, or love, quality can sometimes be easy to recognize or acknowledge, but difficult to define or measure.

Can we believe the results of the trial? This depends on the *internal validity* of the trial, the degree to which the trial design, conduct, analysis, and presentation have minimized or avoided biased comparisons of the interventions being analyzed.

Do the results of the trial apply to us, or to those we wish to help? This is the *external validity*, or *generalizability* of a trial. Are the results sufficiently precise, and the context clearly enough described to tell us if we can apply the results of this randomized controlled trial (RCT) in our setting, to ourselves, or to the people we want to help?

At other times, we may want to focus on the appropriateness of the data analysis, or the way the data are presented.

How can we measure trial quality?

Many of the qualities we have noted (such as the relevance of the research question, the generalizability of the results, the adequacy of data analysis and presentation, and the ethical implications) depend on the context in which they are assessed. Of all the aspects of a trial that have been used to define and assess quality, internal validity is the least context dependent and, as far as we know, the only one that has been the subject of the few empirical studies available. Because of this, we strongly recommend that any assessment of the quality of a trial includes elements related to internal validity. These may, and should, be complemented with other aspects of the trial that may be relevant to one's specific circumstances.

Consider, for example, a trial in which a new antidepressant has been studied in affluent men with suicidal ideation, and shown to reduce suicide rates. The generalizability of the results of this trial would clearly be helpful to a clinician caring for men similar to those who participated in the trial, but would be irrelevant to a peer-reviewer trying to decide whether to recommend the report for publication. The internal validity of the trial, however, would be important to both. Thus, internal validity is an essential component of any assessment of trial quality, even though alone it is not sufficient to provide a comprehensive evaluation.

We now have an increasing number of tools to assess trial quality, but there is little empirical evidence to help us choose among them, or even to evaluate the effect of incorporating quality assessments into reviews and decisions. There is also little empirical evidence on who should do the assessments (number and background of assessors), on how the assessments should be done (e.g. masked versus open conditions), or on the impact of the assessments on health care decisions. The selection of a quality assessment tool may have a profound effect on the conclusions that would be reached from a body of research.[1]

We are hindered in our assessment of trial quality by the need, almost always, to rely on information contained in the written report of an RCT. Unfortunately, a trial with a biased design that is well reported could be judged as having high quality, while a well-designed but poorly reported trial could be judged as having low quality.[2]

In this chapter, we will discuss the barriers to quality assessment, and present the results of empirical methodological studies that could help to overcome them. We will also discuss recent efforts to improve the quality of reports of RCTs, and identify areas where further methodological research is required. We hope that the information in this chapter will be of help to both clinicians and patients trying to decide whether to make use of an intervention, and readers of a systematic review who want to evaluate the effect that the assessment of trial quality may have had on the results of the review (Chapter 6).

What type of tools can be used to assess trial quality?

In order to assess the quality of a trial, we have to select a tool to generate the assessment. At this point we can either develop our own tool or use an existing one.

How can we develop a new tool to assess trial quality?

To develop our own tool, we could simply select a single item or a group of items that we (and perhaps a group of our colleagues) regard as important, decide how to score each item, and use the tool straightaway. For example, after deciding to focus on internal and external validity, we could select 'concealment of allocation' as the item for internal validity and 'description of the setting' as the marker for external validity. We could then decide on our own, or after discussion with our colleagues, to assign 2 points to a trial with adequate concealment and 1 point each for description of the setting. Once we have the items and the scoring system, we can just apply them to trials and obtain scores that would reflect their quality (by our criteria).

The advantage of this approach is that it is relatively simple and always yields a numerical score. The disadvantage is that tools created in this informal way can produce variable assessments of the same trial when used by different raters, and may not adequately discriminate between studies with good, and those with poor quality.

Alternatively, we could develop the new tool following established methodological procedures, similar to those used in the formal development of any other type of health measurement tool. The advantages of this approach are that it is systematic, it can be replicated by others (if we describe it properly), and it can yield a tool with known reliability and construct validity, which would allow readers to discriminate among trials of varied quality. A detailed description of these procedures is beyond the scope of this book, but can be found elsewhere.[3] The following is a list of the steps required to develop a new tool to formally assess trial quality:

- *Definition of the construct 'quality'* (as described in the previous section).
- *Definition of the scope of the tool*: For instance, the tool could be condition specific (e.g. to assess only the quality of trials in obstetrics) or intervention specific (e.g. to assess trials evaluating different types of episiotomies).
- *Definition of the population of end users*: The tool could be designed for use by, for example, clinicians, statisticians or patients, or by individuals with any background.
- *Selection of candidate items to include in the tool*: Usually, this is achieved by asking a group of individuals to propose items to include in the tool, selecting them from items in existing tools or using their own judgment and expertise.
- *Development of a prototype tool*: This is usually achieved by getting the individuals who proposed items to meet and decide, by consensus, on the essential group of items that should be included in

the tool. At this point, the group can also decide on the wording of each item and on a scoring system. The prototype could be tested by using it to score a small group of trials and using the experience gathered during the process to refine the wording and modify the order in which the items are presented.

- *Selection of targets*: Once a prototype tool has been developed, the developers should select a group of trials to be assessed using the tool. These trials should have different degrees of perceived quality (i.e. some should be regarded as having poor quality, while others should be regarded as having high quality).

- *Selection of raters*: The developers should select a group of individuals to use the tool to score the target trials. The characteristics of these individuals should reflect the potential users of the tool.

- *Assessment of the trials*: The trials are given to the raters to assess. These raters could be experienced or naïve to the use of the tool.

- *Evaluation of the consistency of the assessments*: This involves measurement of the degree to which different raters agree on the quality of the trials. This is called *inter-observer* or *inter-rater reliability*. *Reliability* is also referred to as consistency or agreement. Sometimes this also includes an evaluation of the degree of *intra-observer* or *intra-rater reliability*, which refers to the degree of agreement among quality assessments done by the same raters on separate occasions. There are several methods to measure the consistency of the measurements (e.g. percentage agreement, kappa, correlation coefficient, intra-class correlation coefficient). A description of these methods and their advantages and limitations are described elsewhere.[3]

- *Evaluation of 'construct' validity*: *Construct validity* refers to the ability of the tool to measure what it is believed to be measuring. One important limitation to the evaluation of the *construct validity* of a tool to assess trial quality is the lack of a gold standard. To overcome this limitation, the developers usually have to make predictions on how the tool would rate trials previously judged as having different quality and testing these predictions. In this case, you would expect the tool to differentiate between the trials previously judged as having poor quality and those judged as having good quality.

- *Proposal of a refined tool*: Once the tool is shown to be reliable and valid, it is ready for use, and should be reported in the literature.

The main disadvantage of developing a new tool is that it is a time-consuming process. To avoid the need to create one without proper evaluation, or the difficulty of developing a new tool using the established methodology, we can select an existing tool.

What kinds of tools exist to evaluate trial quality?

Existing tools to assess trial quality can be classified broadly into those that include individual components and those that include groups of components.

A component is an item that describes a single aspect of quality. Assessing trial quality using a component can be achieved either by scoring the component as present or absent, or by judging the adequacy of the information available about it. For example, concealment of patient allocation could be judged as present or absent, or it could be judged as adequate, unclear, or inadequate.[4] There are empirical studies showing a relationship between several specific methodological aspects of trials and the likelihood of bias (Chapter 3). These studies suggest that trials with inadequate randomization or double-blinding, those with inadequate or unclear concealment of allocation, and those that inappropriately use cross-over designs, are more likely to produce larger treatment effects than those obtained by their counterparts.[5–7] There is also evidence suggesting that reports of trials sponsored by pharmaceutical companies are more likely to favor the experimental intervention over controls than trials not sponsored by pharmaceutical companies.[8–10] Even though individual components are quick and easy to score, we cannot recommend their use, because they provide minimal information about the overall quality of trials.

The narrow view provided by individual components can be overcome by using several components grouped in checklists or scales. The main difference between a checklist and a scale is that in a checklist, the components are evaluated separately and do not have numerical scores attached to them, while in a scale, each item is scored numerically and an overall quality score is generated. A systematic search of the literature in 1996 identified 9 checklists and 25 scales for assessing trial quality.[11] Ongoing efforts to update this literature search suggest that there are now at least twice as many scales to assess trial quality and that their number is likely to keep increasing.[12] Among the available checklists and scales, only a handful have been developed using established methodological procedures.

What are the validated tools to assess trial quality?

The Jadad scale

This tool was validated by one of us (ARJ) using the steps outlined in the previous sections as part of his doctoral work in pain relief (see Figure 4.1).[13] Since its development, the scale has been used by other investigators who have confirmed that it is easy and quick to use (it takes less than 5 minutes to score a trial report), provides consistent measurements (even those provided by consumers with no health care background), and has construct validity.[14] Although some concerns have been expressed about the inter-observer reliability of the assessments,[15,16] the scale has been cited over 1500 times and has been used successfully to identify systematic differences in over 300 reviews of trials in many areas of health care.

The scale includes three items that are directly related to bias reduction: randomization, blinding, and description of withdrawals and drop outs. These are presented as questions to elicit 'yes' or 'no' answers (Figure 4.1). The scale produces scores from 0 to 5. Points are awarded for positive (yes) answers to each question.

For the first two items (randomization and double-blinding) points awarded depend first on whether the trial is described as randomized or double-blind, and second on the appropriateness of the methods used to randomize and blind the trial. A trial would be awarded 1 point for being described as randomized, and a second point if it also reports the methods used to generate the randomization sequence and they are appropriate. It would get 1 point if it

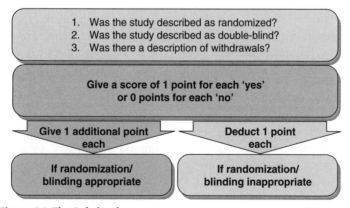

Figure 4.1 The Jadad scale

was described as double-blind, and a second point if the methods to achieve blinded conditions are described and are appropriate.

Thus a trial that is reported as randomized and double-blind, but with no description of the randomization process or of the double-blind conditions would receive 2 points. If the methods of generating the randomization sequence or creating blinded conditions are described and are appropriate, they would receive an additional point for each item. Conversely, if the methods described are inappropriate, 1 point would be deducted for each item; if the methods used to achieve randomization or blinding were not appropriate, the study would receive 0 points for that component.

The third item of the scale, withdrawals and drop outs, is awarded 0 points if they are not reported, and 1 point if they are. For a positive answer, *the number* of withdrawals and drop outs *in each group **and** the reasons* must be stated in the report. If there were no withdrawals, this should also be stated (Figure 4.1). If a trial provides the number *and* reasons for withdrawals and drop outs in each group the reader could re-analyze the data.

A trial could be judged as having poor quality if it is awarded 2 points or less. Studies that obtain 2 or less points have been shown to produce treatment effects which are 35% larger, on average, than those produced by trials with 3 or more points.[17]

It is not always best to use the overall score produced by the scale; sometimes it is more appropriate to use individual items. This is the best option if, for any reason, we do not feel comfortable with lumping different aspects of a trial into a single score, or when the reports describe trials for which double-blinding is not feasible or appropriate (e.g. surgical trials). However, even trials that cannot be double-blind can still be awarded more than 2 points, if they were conducted and reported properly. They could still be awarded 3 points if the reports included a description of appropriate methods to generate the randomization sequence (2 points) and a detailed account of the number *and* the reasons for withdrawals and drop outs in each study group (1 point).

The Jadad scale is not the only, or always most appropriate, way to assess trial quality, but it is the most widely used, and appears to produce robust and valid results in an increasing number of empirical studies. It should not, however, be used in isolation. It should always be complemented with separate assessments of any components for which there is empirical evidence of a direct relationship with bias. Separate assessments of components related to other aspects of trial quality (e.g. external validity, quality of data analysis or presentation, sources of funding, language of publication, country of publication, and, when applicable, the appropriateness of cross-over design) should also be considered.

Delphi-based tools

Two tools have been developed following a Delphi consensus-building process. Both were designed with input from prominent methodologists. One of the tools, developed by a group of nurses at Oxford, consists of 53 items organized in 15 different dimensions,[18] while the other, developed at the University of Maastricht, includes only 9 items.[19] Neither is extensively used today.

The PEDro scale

This scale was designed to assess the quality of trials in physiotherapy.[20] It includes 11 items that derive from the Verhagen scale. Ten of the items are assessed in terms of whether they are present in the article ('yes') or not, and given 1 point for each affirmative answer, for a total score of 10 points. This tool has been shown to provide more consistent results than the Jadad scale during the assessment of trials on physical therapy.[21]

Downs and Black checklist

This is a rarely used tool designed for the assessment of the quality of both randomized and non-randomized studies.[22] It includes 21 items, 10 of which relate to quality of reporting and 17 to external validity.

How and by whom should the assessments be done?

A suggestion was made more than 20 years ago to assess the quality of trial reports under masked conditions, that is, without knowledge of the authors, institutions, sponsorship, publication year and journal, or study results.[5] However, there are only two published empirical studies that address this issue.[23,24] Both of these studies showed that assessments under masked conditions were more likely to yield lower and more consistent scores than assessments under open conditions.

These results imply that bias could be introduced by open assessments. There is, however, evidence suggesting that the differences in the scores obtained under open or masked conditions may not be very important.[23] Masking the reports would reduce the likelihood of bias marginally, but it would also increase the resources required to conduct the assessments. Given the methodological and financial implications of these findings, and the little empirical evidence available, we do not currently recommend that masking the trial reports should be a mandatory step during the assessment of their quality.

We must also consider the number and background of the people required to assess the quality of a given trial. For a clinician trying to keep up to date, this is not an issue, but when we read a systematic review done by others, we may want to see if the authors provide information on who assessed trial quality, and how they assessed it. Typically, systematic reviewers ask two individuals (called raters, observers, or assessors) to assess the trials independently. They are given copies of the trial reports, the assessment instrument(s) with instructions, and a form on which to complete the assessments. The purpose of using more than one individual to assess trial quality is to both minimize the number of mistakes (usually due to oversight while reading the trial report) and the risk of bias during the assessments. Once they have completed the assessments, the raters are invited to meet to discuss their findings and agree on a single quality assessment for each trial. Reaching agreement on trial quality is usually easy, but on occasions it may require a third person to act as arbiter. The degree of agreement between the raters can be quantified using methods described elsewhere.[3]

How can the quality assessments be used?

Once we have assessed the quality of one or more trials, we should use the assessments to guide our decisions. How we use the assessments, however, will depend on why we are assessing the trials, and the number of trials on the same topic to evaluate. We may want to use the assessments to judge whether the results of a trial are credible and applicable to patients; to decide whether a report should be published; to decide whether a new trial is justified or, if justified, to improve its design.

The situation is more complicated if we are reading or conducting a review of several trials on the same topic. In this case, although there are a number of different approaches that could be used to incorporate quality assessments,[7,25] there is little research evidence evaluating the impact of any of these methods on the results of the reviews.

Recent efforts to improve the quality of reporting of RCTs

A major barrier hindering the assessment of trial quality is that in most cases we must rely on the information contained in the written report. The problem is that a trial with a biased design that is well reported could be judged as having high quality, while a well-designed but poorly reported trial could be judged as having low quality. If we contact the authors of the report directly, they may be able to provide the missing information that we require to complete the quality assessments, but they may not have such information available, or they may give us false information. Ideally, all these problems could be avoided if the authors of trial reports provided enough information for the readers to judge whether the results of the trials are reliable.

In 1996, a group of clinical epidemiologists, biostatisticians and journal editors published a statement called CONSORT (Consolidation of the Standards of Reporting Trials) that resulted from an extensive collaborative process the aim of which was to improve the standard of written reports of RCTs.[26,27] The CONSORT statement was designed to assist the reporting of RCTs with two groups and parallel designs. Over the following decade, some modifications were required, to make the instructions clearer, and to enable reporting of cross-over trials and those with more than two groups.[28,29]

The latest version of the CONSORT statement includes a checklist of 22 items and a four-stage flow diagram for use by the authors to provide journal editors and peer-reviewers with the page of the report in which each of the items is addressed. The flowchart provides a detailed description of the progress of participants through the randomized trial, from the number of potentially eligible individuals for inclusion in the trial to the number of trial participants in each group who completed the trial. Each of the items in the checklist and the elements of the flowchart will be described in detail in Chapter 5.

Will the quality of RCTs improve?

Soon after its publication, the CONSORT statement was endorsed by major journals such as the *British Medical Journal*, *The Lancet*, the *Journal of the American Medical Association*, and the *Canadian Medical Association Journal*. These journals incorporated the CONSORT statement as part of the requirements for authors from

January 1, 1997. Within 6 months of the publication of the state-ment, another 30 journals endorsed it, as well as the International Committee of Medical Journal Editors.

Although the CONSORT statement was not evaluated before its publication, a systematic review of methodologically weak studies has shown that journals that adopt it had significantly better report-ing of the method of sequence generation, allocation concealment, and overall number of CONSORT items, not only compared with baseline, but also with non-adopters. Unfortunately, the number of journals that have endorsed CONSORT and those that comply with it, after endorsing it, remain low.

Our musings

We have been developing and using tools to assess the quality of clinical trials for over 20 years. It is certainly reasonable to believe that a high-quality trial will provide better information, and a bet-ter guide to practice, than one of low quality. But for the present, this is an unsubstantiated belief. To date it remains unclear whether the assessment of trial quality is necessary, possible, or benefi-cial. Most of the few validated tools are rarely used. The tool that leads the pack, the Jadad scale, has become a staple of systematic reviews, despite its narrow scope and the dearth of evidence of ben-efit beyond early studies that attributed to it the potential to identify distortion of effects by trials deemed to have low quality.

The rapid proliferation of non-validated quality assessment tools is not helping; rather it is compounding the problem. They have been appearing too quickly to be replicated or monitored. The only requirements for their publication seem to be an author with imag-ination and an eager journal editor.

As our understanding of trials and their proper place in the con-tinuum of evidence to guide practice increases, we can hope for perhaps fewer, but better, RCTs to guide us in the future.

References

1. Juni P, Witschi A, Bloch R, Egger M. The hazards of scoring the quality of clinical trials for meta-analysis. *Journal of American Medical Association* 1999;282:1054–1060.
2. Hill CL, LaValley MP, Felson DT. Discrepancy between published report and actual conduct of randomized clinical trials. *Journal of Clinical Epidemiology* 2002;55:783–786.

3. Streiner DL, Norman GR. *Health Measurement Scales: A Practical Guide to Their Development and Use*, 3rd edition. Oxford: Oxford University Press, 2003.

4. Schulz KF, Chalmers I, Hayes RJ, Altman DG. Empirical evidence of bias: dimensions of methodological quality associated with estimates of treatment effect in controlled clinical trials. *Journal of American Medical Association* 1995;273:408–412.

5. Chalmers TC, Celano P, Sacks HS, Smith H. Bias in treatment assignment in controlled clinical trials. *New England Journal of Medicine* 1983;309:1359–1361.

6. Colditz GA, Miller JN, Mosteller F. How study design affects outcomes in comparisons of therapy. I. Therapy. *Statistics in Medicine* 1989;8:441–454.

7. Khan KS, Daya S, Jadad AR. The importance of quality of primary studies in producing unbiased systematic reviews. *Archives of Internal Medicine* 1996;156:661–666.

8. Cho MK, Bero LA. The quality of drug studies published in symposium proceedings. *Annals of Internal Medicine* 1996;124:485–488.

9. Yaphe J, Edman R, Knishkowy B, Herman J. The association between funding by commercial interests and study outcome in randomized controlled drug trials. *Family Practice* 2001;18:565–568.

10. Bhandari M, Busse JW, Jackowski D, Montori VM, Schunemann H, Sprague S, Mears D, Schemitsch EH, Heels-Ansdell D, Devereaux PJ. Association between industry funding and statistically significant pro-industry findings in medical and surgical randomized trials. *Canadian Medical Association Journal* 2004;170:477–480.

11. Moher D, Jadad AR, Nichol G, Penman M, Tugwell P, Walsh S. Assessing the quality of randomized controlled trials: an annotated bibliography of scales and checklists. *Controlled Clinical Trials* 1995;16:62–73.

12. Moher D, Cook DJ, Jadad AR, Tugwell P, Moher M, Jones A, Pham B, Klassen TP. Assessing the quality of reports of randomised trials: implications for the conduct of meta-analyses. *Health Technology Assessment* 1999;3:1–98.

13. Jadad AR. Meta-analysis of randomized clinical trials in pain relief. D. Phil Thesis, University of Oxford, 1994.

14. Ohlsson A, Lacy JB. Quality assessments of randomized controlled trials: an evaluation by the Chalmers versus the Jadad method. *3rd Annual Cochrane Colloquium* 1995:V9–V10.

15. Clark HD, Wells GA, Huet C, McAlister FA, Salmi LR, Fergusson D, Laupacis A. Assessing the quality of randomized trials: reliability of the Jadad scale. *Controlled Clinical Trials* 1999;20:448–452.

16. Bhandari M, Richards RR, Sprague S, Schemitsch EH. Quality in the reporting of randomized trials in surgery: Is the Jadad scale reliable? *Controlled Clinical Trials* 2001;22:687–688.

17. Moher D, Jones A, Cook DJ, Jadad AR, Moher M, Tugwell P, Klassen TP. Does quality of reports of randomised trials affect estimates of intervention efficacy reported in meta-analyses? *Lancet* 1998;352:609–613.
18. Sindhu F, Carpenter L, Seers K. Development of a tool to rate the quality assessment of randomized controlled trials using a Delphi technique. *Journal of Advanced Nursing* 1997;25:1262–1268.
19. Verhagen AP, de Vet HC, de Bie RA, Kessels AG, Boers M, Bouter LM, Knipschild PG. The Delphi list: a criteria list for quality assessment of randomized clinical trials for conducting systematic reviews developed by Delphi consensus. *Journal of Clinical Epidemiology* 1998;51:1235–1241.
20. Maher CG, Sherrington C, Herbert RD, Moseley AM, Elkins M. Reliability of the PEDro scale for rating quality of randomized controlled trials. *Physical Therapy* 2003;83:713–721.
21. Bhogal SK, Teasell RW, Foley NC, Speechley MR. The PEDro scale provides a more comprehensive measure of methodological quality than the Jadad scale in stroke rehabilitation literature. *Journal of Clinical Epidemiology* 2005;58:668–673.
22. Downs SH, Black N. The feasibility of creating a checklist for the assessment of the methodological quality both of randomised and non-randomised studies of health care interventions. *Journal of Epidemiology and Community Health* 1998;52:377–384.
23. Berlin JA for the University of Pennsylvania Meta-analysis Blinding Study Group. Does blinding of readers affect the results of meta-analyses? *Lancet* 1997;350:185–186.
24. Detsky AS, Naylor CD, O'Rourke K, McGeer AJ, L'Abbe KA. Incorporating variations in the quality of individual randomized trials into meta-analysis. *Journal of Clinical Epidemiology* 1992;45:255–265.
25. Moher D, Jadad AR, Tugwell P. Assessing the quality of randomized controlled trials. *International Journal of Technology Assessment in Health Care* 1996;12:195–208.
26. Begg C, Cho M, Eastwood S, Horton R, Moher D, Olkin I, Pitkin R, Rennie D, Schulz KF, Simel D, Stroup D. Improving the quality of reporting of randomized controlled trials – the CONSORT statement. *Journal of American Medical Association* 1996;276:637–639.
27. Altman DG. Better reporting of randomised controlled trials: the CONSORT statement. *British Medical Journal* 1996;313:570–571.
28. Moher D, Altman DG, Schulz KF, Elbourne DR. Opportunities and challenges for improving the quality of reporting clinical research: CONSORT and beyond. *Canadian Medical Association Journal* 2004;171:349–350.
29. Plint AC, Moher D, Morrison A, Schulz K, Altman DG, Hill C, Gaboury I. Does the CONSORT checklist improve the quality of reports of randomised controlled trials? A systematic review. *Medical Journal of Australia* 2006;185:263–267.

CHAPTER 5

Reporting and interpreting individual trials: the essentials

The way in which we interpret the results of a trial depends on several closely related factors, including our understanding of the value and limitations of trial reports as sources of information to guide decisions in health care and the amount and clarity of the information we find in the trial reports.

Additional factors such as the extent to which we are familiar with the content area addressed by the trial, our understanding of the principles of data analysis and statistics, the time we have to read the trial report, and our level of awareness about our personal biases and how they could affect what we will find in the report, inevitably vary from person to person, and are beyond the scope of this book.

The relation between trial reporting and interpretation

In most cases, the only information that we have to help us to interpret a trial is its published report. Unfortunately, evidence generated during the past 30 years has repeatedly demonstrated the wide gap between what a trial should report to help readers interpret its results, and what is actually published.[1] Most reports do not contain all the information that we require to make informed judgments on the internal and external validity of the trials reported.

As we mentioned in the previous chapter, in 1996 an international group of clinical epidemiologists, biostatisticians, and journal editors published a statement called CONSORT (CONsolidation of the Standards Of Reporting Trials),[1] the aim of which was to improve the standards of written reports of randomized controlled trials (RCTs) and to ensure that readers find in the reports all the information they require to interpret the trial results with confidence. This statement, which has been modified over the past decade[2,3] now includes a checklist of 22 items (Table 5.1) and a flow diagram that authors should use to provide information on the progress of patients through a study (Figure 5.1). Updates and news about CONSORT are available at http://www.consort-statement.org/.

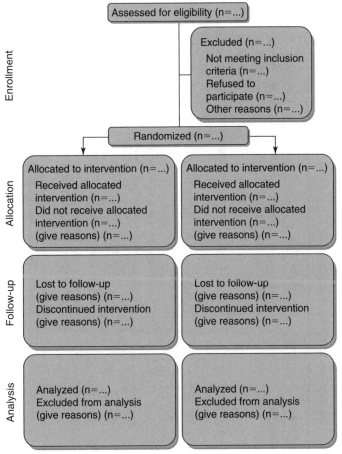

Figure 5.1 Flow diagram of subject progress through the phases of a randomized trial (Reprinted from Moher et al., 2001. *Journal of American Medical Association*, with permission. See Ref. [2])

Table 5.1 Checklist of the CONSORT Statement for trials with parallel group design (Opportunities and challenges for improving the quality of reporting clinical research: CONSORT and beyond "Reprinted from *CMAJ* 17-Aug-04; 171(4) Pages 349–350 by permission of the publisher. © 2004 Canadian Medical Association.)

Section and topic	Item#	Descriptor	Reported on page #
Title and abstract	1	How participants were allocated to interventions (e.g. "random allocation," "randomised," or "randomly assigned").	
Introduction			
Background	2	Scientific background and explanation of rationale.	
Methods			
Participants	3	Eligibility criteria for participants and the settings and locations where the data were collected.	
Interventions	4	Precise details of the interventions intended for each group and how and when they were actually administered.	
Objectives	5	Specific objectives and hypotheses.	
Outcomes	6	Clearly defined primary and secondary outcome measures and, when applicable, any methods used to enhance the quality of measurements (e.g. multiple observations, training of assessors).	
Sample size	7	How sample size was determined and, when applicable, explanation of any interim analyses and stopping rules.	

Randomization

Sequence generation	8	Method used to generate the random allocation sequence, including details of any restriction (e.g. blocking, stratification).
Allocation concealment	9	Method used to implement the random allocation sequence (e.g. numbered containers or central telephone), clarifying whether the sequence was concealed until interventions were assigned.
Implementation	10	Who generated the allocation sequence, who enrolled participants, and who assigned participants to their groups.
Blinding (masking)	11	Whether or not participants, those administering the interventions, and those assessing the outcomes were blinded to group assignment. If done, how the success of blinding was evaluated.
Statistical methods	12	Statistical methods used to compare groups for primary outcome(s); methods for additional analyses, such as subgroup analyses and adjusted analyses.

Results

Participant flow	13	Flow of participants through each stage (a diagram is strongly recommended). Specifically, for each group report the numbers of participants randomly assigned, receiving intended treatment, completing the study protocol, and analyzed for the primary outcome. Describe protocol deviations from study as planned, together with reasons.
Recruitment	14	Dates defining the periods of recruitment and follow-up.
Baseline data	15	Baseline demographic and clinical characteristics of each group.

Continued

Table 5.1 (*Continued*)

Section and topic	Item#	Descriptor	Reported on page #
Numbers analyzed	16	Number of participants (denominator) in each group included in each analysis and whether the analysis was by "intention-to-treat." State the results in absolute numbers when feasible (e.g. 10/20, not 50%).	
Outcomes and estimation	17	For each primary and secondary outcome, a summary of results for each group, and the estimated effect size and its precision (e.g. 95% confidence interval).	
Ancillary analyses	18	Address multiplicity by reporting any other analyses performed, including subgroup analyses and adjusted analyses, indicating those prespecified and those exploratory.	
Adverse events	19	All important adverse events or side effects in each intervention group.	
Comment Interpretation	20	Interpretation of the results, taking into account study hypotheses, sources of potential bias or imprecision, and the dangers associated with multiplicity of analyses and outcomes.	
Generalizability	21	Generalizability (external validity) of the trial findings.	
Overall evidence	22	General interpretation of the results in the context of current evidence.	

The original article and the sequels in which the CONSORT statement was described, however, were short and targeted *authors* of trial reports *rather than readers*. In this chapter, we will use the CONSORT statement as a template to describe the elements that should be taken into account when *reading* a trial report to interpret its results. We will also use information from our own experience as readers, and from two recent books on how to read articles and on how to teach and practice evidence-based medicine.[4,5]

Our main challenge in writing this chapter was to keep the discussion of the issues brief and clear, focusing on the essential elements that readers need to take into account when interpreting the results of an RCT report. Our aim is to help make efficient use of the limited time that can be spent reading articles. When appropriate, we expand on issues discussed in previous chapters or refer directly to the sections of the book where certain items have been discussed in more detail. In addition, we include one or more additional sources of information where we can find detailed explanations of specific issues, particularly statistical ones, which are beyond the scope of this book.

What are the key elements of a trial report needed to interpret its results with confidence?

To interpret the results of a trial with confidence, regardless of our background, the time we have available to read a trial report and the reasons why we are reading it, we will have to answer at least the following questions:

- Is the topic interesting?
- Are the results likely to be unbiased?
- Would I be able to use the results?
- Are the results important enough for me to remember?

In the rest of this chapter, we will try to answer these questions in a way that would allow readers to address them in a time-efficient manner, and point out the sections of a report in which the information needed is most likely to be found.

We may focus on different aspects of a report depending on why we are reading it. We could be considering an intervention to treat a specific patient, to design a new RCT, to judge whether a trial report should be published in a journal, to conduct a systematic review of multiple trials, to purchase a service or a new intervention, or only to scan what is written in the latest issue of a journal.

Although we will do our best to provide enough information to answer any of the above questions regardless of the circumstances, we have focused primarily on meeting the needs of busy clinicians, researchers, and patients, who have limited experience in methodology and research.

Is the topic addressed by the trial interesting?

The answer to this question will depend on our background and on the degree to which the trial is likely to meet our immediate needs. For instance, a trial entitled 'The use of therapeutic touch for the treatment of malignant melanoma' is likely to be interesting to an oncologist, to someone whose loved one has a melanoma, to an individual involved in decisions about providing services for patients with melanoma, or to a journalist who writes about health issues. It is less likely to be interesting to a cardiologist.

Usually, all one has to do to decide if a report is interesting is to look at its title. If by reading the title we do not think that the article is interesting, we should either move on to another article or do something else.[5] In the rare event that we cannot find enough information in the title of a report to decide whether or not it is interesting to us, we would likely find this out in the first portion of the abstract or in the introduction of the report.

After reading the title of the article, if it seems interesting, we might feel tempted to jump to the conclusions in the abstract. This may occur because of our irresistible curiosity to know the 'bottom line' of the article, because we are so busy that reading the title and parts of the abstract is all we have time for, or because we don't want to know anything else even if we did have enough time to read the whole article. We should resist this temptation, because the information in the title and the abstract could give us a misleading message. We should use the information in the abstract just as an additional source of information to determine if the trial is interesting to us (unless we are reading journals containing only structured abstracts of high-quality studies published elsewhere, as we discuss in Chapter 7).

The main message at this point is that we should resist the temptation to use only the information provided by the abstract of an original study to make decisions about patient care, or anything else that is important.

Are the trial results likely to be unbiased?

After spending a couple of minutes reading the title and the abstract of the trial report, if we decide that the article is still interesting, we should try to decide whether the trial is of good methodological quality (Chapter 4).

It should take approximately 3 to 5 minutes to assess the quality of a trial report. With experience it could take less than 1 minute, particularly if the authors have included methodological information in the title and in the abstract.

Authors of RCT reports can help us find the information we need easily, if they follow simple approaches to make the titles of their reports as informative as possible. For instance, we would have no problem in finding the information we need if the authors of the report have followed an approach that has been used extensively by journals such as *ACP Journal Club* and *Evidence-Based Medicine*, two journals that have been designed to help readers access high-quality information efficiently (Chapter 7). Using this approach, efforts are made to create informative titles that tell us something not only about the topic addressed by the trial, but also about its design and results. For instance, a more informative title for the hypothetical trial on therapeutic touch for the treatment of melanoma could be *'Therapeutic touch as a supplement to surgery can increase survival in patients with grade II melanoma: a randomized double-blind trial'*.

The abstracts of RCT reports should ideally be structured, including a systematic disclosure of the objective, research design, clinical setting, participants, interventions, main outcome measures, results, and conclusions.[6] Ideally, an abstract should contain enough information to let us judge how scientifically sound the trial is likely to be, and how relevant its results may be to our immediate needs. If the abstract is informative enough, the information it contains should be sufficient to allow us to decide whether we should read more of the article or look at another one.

As we emphasized earlier, regardless of how informative an abstract is, we should resist the temptation to use only the information provided there to make decisions about patient care. If, based on the information in the title and abstract, we think that the trial is neither scientifically sound nor relevant to us, then we should stop reading it and, if appropriate, move to another report.

Sometimes we may think that the trial is not scientifically sound, but the topic is very interesting to us. In these cases, the decision as to whether to read the whole report or not should depend on the amount of additional literature available on the same topic. If we are aware of other, possibly more sound, trials addressing the same issue, then we could stop reading the report we just found. However, if we do not know of any other trial, we may want to read the whole report very carefully, and make efforts to extract as much usable information as possible. On most occasions, however, trials that are not scientifically strong should be regarded as generators of hypotheses that we or others could test under more rigorous conditions.

If, based on the information on the title and abstract, we think that the trial is likely to be scientifically sound and relevant, we could decide to read the whole article from beginning to end, or to read specific components of the report in a systematic manner. By doing this we can confirm that the trial is as scientifically sound and interesting as the title and abstract suggest, and can also determine whether we could use the results.

How can we determine if we would be able to use the results of a trial?

RCTs, even if perfectly designed, can tell us which treatment is better on average, but they cannot tell us for whom it is better. How and whether to generalize the results of an individual trial to an individual patient is one of the most complex issues in health care.[7,8] Perhaps the only situation in which we could apply the results of a trial to an individual confidently is when we have done an n-of-1 trial on that individual (Chapter 2). Otherwise, we are left with information from a group of other patients, studied by others, in other settings. In this case, we should try to determine the extent to which the research question of the trial matches our own questions, and how satisfied we feel about this based on the information available in the report about the execution and results of the trial.

Does the research question match our own questions?

Although the research question is one of the most important components of a trial and its report, it is frequently overlooked and underestimated by authors, peer-reviewers, and journal editors.

The report should include a clearly identified research question formulated in simple terms, with information on the broad characteristics of the participants (e.g. male adults over 65 years of age), the condition (e.g. grade II melanoma), the setting (e.g. a tertiary level cancer center), the interventions (e.g. surgery alone versus surgery plus therapeutic touch) and the outcomes (e.g. disease-free survival, quality of life).[9] In our example, the research question could be formulated like this:

'*What is the effect of therapeutic touch as a supplement to surgery compared with surgery alone on the survival rate at 5 years of adult patients with grade II melanoma attending a tertiary level cancer center?*'

Unfortunately, we will not find clearly described research questions in most of the reports we read. If we do not find a clear research question, but still think that the trial could be important, we must try to find as much information as possible on the individual elements of the research question in the Abstract, Introduction, and Methods section of the report.

Once we have a better idea of the question or questions that the trial tried to answer, we should look for information on how the trial was executed to establish whether we could use its results.

Does the report include enough information on the execution of the study?

By looking for information on how the trial was carried out, we will be able to assess how well it was executed, and whether we could use its results. To judge the execution of a trial, we should answer the following questions:

• *What was the sampling frame? How did the investigators approach prospective participants?*

The report should provide clear information on the source of prospective participants for the trial and on the methods used to approach them. These two factors are closely related to the unit of allocation. When the unit of allocation or analysis is at the individual study participant level, the *sampling frame* is usually a group of patients attending a given health care institution (e.g. clinic, hospital, community center). When groups of health professionals, special interest groups, or health care institutions themselves are the units of allocation, the sampling frame is usually a geographic area.

The report should mention whether all or just a sub-set of all prospective participants (individuals or groups) were approached. It should also describe whether prospective participants were approached consecutively, randomly or using any other method, and provide at least the number (and ideally the number and reasons) of prospective participants that refused to be considered for the study.

If the unit of analysis of the trial is not at the individual participant level, but at a group or cluster level, the authors should provide a reason for this. In addition, if the trial used cluster randomization (Chapter 2), we should interpret its results carefully if the authors used standard statistical techniques, as these can lead to invalid results.[8]

Ideally, trial reports should describe prospective participants who were invited to take part in the trial, but who refused to participate. This information, however, is found very rarely in trial reports.

In addition to telling us about the sources of prospective participants, the trial report should also describe how prospective participants were approached and recruited into the study. Usual methods to recruit participants include word of mouth, an invitation letter, or an advertisement in a newspaper, or other media. The report should also include information on the body responsible for approving the trial from an ethical perspective (Chapter 8).

- *What criteria were used to include prospective participants in the study?*

The description of the inclusion criteria should provide information on the health status of the participants (e.g. patients with grade II melanoma), their previous exposure to interventions that may influence the results of the trial (e.g. no previous chemotherapy, surgery, or therapeutic touch), and general demographic characteristics that could also influence the effects of the interventions (e.g. age, gender, socio-economic status, educational background, race, religious beliefs, etc.).

The exclusion criteria should also be described in detail and should be justified whenever possible. If the inclusion criteria are described in sufficient specific detail a detailed description of the exclusion criteria would not be needed.

Ideally, a report should include information on the number of prospective participants who were approached by the investigators and met the inclusion criteria, but refused to participate in the study. In addition, the report should include information on prospective participants who were not included in the trial because they did not meet the inclusion criteria.

After we identify the sources of trial participants (the sampling frame discussed in the previous question) and have a clear idea of the criteria used to select or exclude them, we should be able to judge whether the sample studied is close enough to the population that will be affected by our decisions.

- *Was the setting appropriate? Was it similar to our own setting?*

In addition to the characteristics of trial participants, we should try to determine whether the setting where they were studied resembles the setting in which we have to make decisions. Therefore, the report should include information on the place where the interventions were administered (e.g. both surgical resection of the melanotic lesions and therapeutic touch were conducted in a 500-bed tertiary level cancer center affiliated with a faculty of health sciences) and where the outcomes were assessed (e.g. the outcomes were assessed in the outpatient clinics of the same institution).

- *What were the interventions? How and by whom were they given?*

The report should include detailed information on the characteristics of the interventions (e.g. the extent to which the melanotic lesions were resected, the technique for therapeutic touch given to the patients in the experimental group and the 'placebo' therapeutic touch given to patients in the control group), the profile of the individuals in charge of administering them (i.e. the number, level of experience, and training of those performing all the interventions), and the regimens used to administer the interventions (usually, this refers to the number, size, and frequency of the doses of a medication; in the therapeutic touch example, this could refer to the number, duration, and timing of the sessions).

The report should also include information on important co-interventions (e.g. the number of patients in each group who received chemotherapy) that could influence the outcomes of the trial.

- *How were randomization and blinding implemented?*

These two important aspects of a trial were discussed in detail in Chapter 3. In brief, the report should provide information on the method used to generate the allocation sequence, the strategies used to ensure allocation concealment, the level of blinding, and the methods used to blind different individuals during the trial.

A simple way to judge whether randomization was implemented properly is by comparing the distribution of certain characteristics of participants at the beginning of the trial (these are also called the 'baseline' characteristics) across the study groups. If randomization has been successful, there should be no statistical differences among the groups in terms of baseline characteristics thought to influence the effect of the interventions.[8]

- *What were the outcomes of interest? How were they measured?*

The report should identify all outcomes that were measured during the trial, both desirable and adverse. In addition, it should specify the tools used to assess the outcomes, the time in which the outcomes were assessed, and the profile (number and background) of the people in charge of assessing them.

Once we have identified the outcomes and how they were measured, we should find out whether the authors stated which outcome was regarded as the primary one and which outcomes were regarded as secondary. The primary outcome is the main event or condition that the trial was designed to evaluate. If the primary outcome is not specified *a priori* (or, worse still, not specified at all) and all outcomes are treated alike, there is an increased risk for the authors to highlight those with the most striking results. In addition, the more outcomes that are analyzed the greater the risk of finding false-positive, statistically significant results, merely by chance.

- *Were the results of the trial analyzed properly?*

This is one of the most important, complex, and yet frequently underestimated aspects of reading a trial report. Most readers typically skip sections that include statistical information, assuming that the authors, peer-reviewers, and editors have taken care of the details and have ensured that the analyses were perfect. Sometimes, sadly, this is the best that we can do.

Unfortunately, trial reports often do not provide a complete description of the statistical methods used to analyze the results and when they do, the methods are often incorrectly used and applied. Providing a detailed account of the steps and judgments that need to be made when evaluating the statistical aspects of a trial report is beyond the scope of this book and can be found in excellent sources.[10,11]

- *Does the report include enough information on the results of the trial?*

We must always be prepared to find discrepancies between what authors planned to do, what they should have done, and what they actually report in the Results section. In any case, we should expect that the trial report will provide at least the following information:

   - *A profile of the flow of participants throughout the trial:* The trial report should provide enough information for us to fill all the boxes in the flowchart of the CONSORT statement (see Figure 5.1). With this information, we will be able to judge the proportion of eligible participants who were actually enrolled in the trial (this will help us determine the representativeness of the study sample), the proportion of participants who received the interventions as allocated, the adequacy of follow-up, the reasons why some participants were withdrawn from the study, and the number of participants who completed the trial.

- *Description of the point estimates, measures of variability, and probability values for the main outcomes*: Often, we will find that trials report point estimates only in graphs, do not provide measures of variability (e.g. confidence intervals, standard deviations, or standard errors) or do not give the actual probability values (e.g. state that the results were 'statistically significant' rather than the actual value of $p = 0.03$).

Once we address the previous issues and determine whether we could use the results of the trial, we should try to answer the following question.

Is the trial important enough for us to use?

This is another complex question. We can answer it simply by realizing that the importance of a trial and its results are in the eye of the beholder. Our decision in each case is likely to depend on the interaction between the methodological characteristics and content of the trial itself; our own beliefs, values and preferences; and the circumstances in which we are reading the article. In all cases our decision will be influenced by each of the trial characteristics discussed so far, and additional factors such as our interpretation of the importance of the effects of the interventions, both favorable and undesirable, found in the study report.

Our musings

One of the strongest temptations we encounter comes from the excitement we feel when we find a recent trial that has been well executed and reported, and that seems to meet our immediate needs. We must resist the temptation to immediately apply the results because one trial, no matter how interesting, relevant, and well reported, may be just one among many other studies that address the same question, and which may contradict or corroborate the findings of the trial we just found. It is important to set the results of individual trials in the context of other relevant studies and other sources of information.

Efforts to improve the quality of reporting of trials have been disappointing.[12] The meager impact of large-scale, high-profile, and concerted international efforts such as those that led to the CONSORT statement is very concerning, not only in terms of the extremely low levels of adoption among journals, but by the lack compliance even by those that were its initial champions.

There is room for innovation. Even if a report complies perfectly with all of the guidelines and recommendations, there would still be a wide gap between what the investigators planned to do, what they actually did, and how they reported it.13 With the rapid development of the Internet, and the sharp fall in prices for digital storage, journals and other publishing media now have unprecedented opportunities to enrich the information available about a trial. We can envisage a traditional text-based report of a trial being complemented by multi-media available through diverse channels and platforms. For instance, authors could have blogs in which they interact with readers; podcasts could enable interested parties to listen to news related to trial reports on the run; videos of patients describing and sharing their experiences during the trial with their peers; authors could continue to update and improve the information they initially provided, in response to new data or feedback from users.

Although we cannot predict the future of communication technologies, we believe that, even with what we know and have now, trial reports could leap from their current constricting format to become a living source of information with the capacity to evolve.[14,15]

References

1. Begg C, Cho M, Eastwood S, Horton R, Moher D, Olkin I, Pitkin R, Rennie D, Schulz KF, Simel D, Stroup D. Improving the quality of reporting of randomized controlled trials – The CONSORT Statement. *Journal of American Medical Association* 1996;276(63):7–9.
2. Moher D, Jones A, Lepage L. CONSORT Group (Consolidated Standards for Reporting of Trials). Use of the CONSORT statement and quality of reports of randomized trials: a comparative before-and-after evaluation. *Journal of American Medical Association* 2001;285:1992–1995.
3. Moher D, Altman DG, Schulz KF, Elbourne DR. Opportunities and challenges for improving the quality of reporting clinical research: CONSORT and beyond. *Canadian Medical Association Journal* 2004;171:349–350.

4. Guyatt G, Rennie D. User's Guide to the Medical Literature: Essentials of Evidence-Based Clinical Practice. *American Medical Association* 2001.

5. Straus SE, Richardson WS, Glasziou P, Haynes RB. *Evidence Based Medicine: How to Practice and Teach EBM*, 3rd edition. Edinburgh: Churchill Livingstone, 2005.

6. Haynes RB, Mulrow CD, Huth EJ, Altman DG, Gardner MJ. More informative abstracts revisited. *Annals of Internal Medicine* 1990;113:69–76.

7. Bailey, KR. Generalizing the results of randomized clinical trials. *Controlled Clinical Trials* 1994;15:15–23.

8. Altman DG. Comparability of randomized groups. *Statistician* 1985;34:125–136.

9. Richardson W, Wilson M, Nishikawa J, et al. The well-built clinical question: a key to evidence-based decisions. *ACP Journal Club* 1995; 123:12–13.

10. Altman, DG. *Practical Statistics for Medical Research*, 2nd edition. UK: Chapman & Hall, 2006.

11. Norman GR, Streiner DL. *PDQ Statistics*, 3rd edition. Toronto: BC Decker, 2003.

12. Plint AC, Moher D, Morrison A, Schulz K, Altman DG, Hill C, Gaboury I. Does the CONSORT checklist improve the quality of reports of randomised controlled trials? A systematic review. *Medical Journal of Australia* 2006;185:263–267.

13. Latour B. *Science in Action: How to Follow Scientists and Engineers Through Society*. Cambridge, MA: Harvard University Press, 1987.

14. Jadad AR, Enkin M. The new alchemy: transmuting information to knowledge in the electronic age. *Canadian Medical Association Journal* 2000;162:1826–1828.

15. Deshpande A, Jadad AR. Web 2.0: Could it help move the health system into the 21st century? *Journal of Men's Health and Gender* 2006;3:332–336.

CHAPTER 6

From individual trials to groups of trials: reviews, meta-analyses, and guidelines

Often we will find more than one trial that addresses our question or a very similar research question. Because these trials are conducted in different groups of people, in different settings, perform the interventions differently, and are funded by different sources, it is unlikely that they will provide identical results. Sometimes, different trials on the same topic have totally opposite results. On many occasions, a trial may become unduly prominent as a result of large investments by groups with vested interests, whose intentions may not be aligned with what is best for patients.[1] The corollary is that it may be risky to make decisions based on the information from a single trial.

If we want to make decisions based on the best available knowledge, we must not only consider as many trials as possible, but also take other types of information into account (Chapter 7). Identifying and synthesizing the information from all relevant sources to guide a particular decision is not an easy task. In this chapter, we will highlight issues related to the identification of relevant trials, and the role of reviews of multiple trials to guide health-related decisions. As in previous chapters, many of the issues that we will discuss here deserve a chapter on their own, and have been addressed more extensively elsewhere. Our intention in this chapter, as in the rest of the book, is to highlight the most important information and to point to more comprehensive sources when appropriate.

What impedes our identification of all relevant trials on a given topic?

The main problem derives from the speed with which the literature is growing. More than a decade ago it was estimated that over 2 million articles, and more than 17,000 biomedical books are published annually.[2] The growth in the number of scientific journals has been exponential at least since the 18th century, fueled by the profit they generate for the societies and commercial organizations that publish them.[3] The total number of trials that have been completed to date has also been growing exponentially and is thought to be in the hundreds of thousands.[4] In some areas, the time it takes for the number of published trials to double is less than 10 years.[5]

This information 'explosion' is compounded by the fact that there is no single source of information that can provide easy and reliable access to all randomized controlled trials (RCTs) on a given topic. All existing databases are incomplete (one of the main problems being the poor access to unpublished trials) or use coding systems that cannot cope with the diversity of topics in health care.

What is the best source for identifying RCTs?

The Cochrane Central Register of Clinical Trials (formerly known as the Cochrane Controlled Trials Database) is perhaps the most advanced and comprehensive source of RCTs in health care. It contains citations for close to 500,000 citations of controlled trials (it was one-third of that number at the time of the first edition of this book, under a decade ago). These trials were identified through the collective effort of members of the Cochrane Collaboration (see below) to improve the identification of primary studies. They have achieved this through the development of high-yield strategies to search bibliographic databases, augmented by extensive hand searching of journals to identify studies that cannot be identified efficiently by electronic searches or that are not indexed in bibliographic databases. The complete database is available on CD-ROM (updated four times a year) and online, free in many countries around the world.[6]

Other sources of published trials that we could use include traditional bibliographic databases such as MEDLINE[7] or EMBASE.[8] During the past decade, as the Internet has been growing and developing, many efforts have emerged to enable easy access to ongoing clinical trials.[9]

Even if we were able to identify citations for all the studies we require to inform a particular decision, it would be hard to find the time required to obtain hard copies of the articles and to read them. Sometimes, key articles are published in languages that we may not understand. We would have to ignore them or invest resources to translate them. These problems would be almost insurmountable if we tried to find all this information on our own. Fortunately, other options are available to facilitate our efforts to identify and synthesize multiple trials.

Are there easier ways to find and use multiple RCTs?

One of the options is to read a summary prepared by others, relying on those who have already spent time, money, and energy to summarize information from multiple trials on relevant topics or even entire specialties. One exemplar of these efforts is known as BMJ Updates, an online initiative spearheaded by the Health Information Research Unit at McMaster University in Canada in collaboration with the *British Medical Journal*.[10] A team of information specialists scan over 100 journals every month, identifying those reports of studies that have a low likelihood of bias. Such reports are then sent to a group of clinicians, who rate them in terms of their relevance and newsworthiness, using a scale ranging from 1 to 7, and include valuable notes for the readers. This system allows setting up an automatic delivery of articles in most specialties, by e-mail, without charge.

What are the different types of reviews?

Because of the rapid expansion of the literature and the progressive compression of our time and resources, review articles are becoming increasingly attractive as tools to guide health care decisions. As with any other tools, reviews can be well built or defective, and can be used well, or abused.

Traditionally, there have been two major types of reviews: narrative and systematic. During the past decade, there has been an explosion of new approaches that recognize the complexity of trying to make sense of a rapidly growing body of literature that crosses disciplinary, conceptual, theoretical, geographic, and thematic boundaries.[11] In this chapter, we will discuss some general principles of reviews, but will focus on reviews of RCTs using traditional approaches. In Chapter 7, we will introduce the relationship between RCTs and other study designs, as well as other sources of information.

What is a narrative review?

A narrative review is the typical review article that we find in most journals.[12] These reviews are produced by individuals, often experts in their field, using informal and subjective methods to collect and interpret information. They are appealing to those who write them, because they are relatively easy and quick to produce, and attractive to readers because they distill the views of an authority in a short piece. The problem remains that they are idiosyncratic and cannot be replicated by others. They have been shown to sometimes be incomplete[13] and likely to be a biased reflection of the opinions of the authors.[14] They may also delay the identification of effective or harmful interventions by 10–15 years, when compared with more systematic approaches to reviewing the literature.[15,16]

What is a systematic review?

A systematic review, in its ideal form, is a review that includes an explicit and detailed description of how it was conducted, such that any interested reader would be able to replicate it. In its purest form, the report of a systematic review should include a clear research question, criteria for inclusion or exclusion of primary studies, the process used to identify primary studies, the methods used to assess the methodological quality of the selected studies, and the methods used to extract and summarize the results of primary trials on which the conclusions are based.[17,18] Systematic reviews overcome many of the limitations of narrative reviews, although they require more time and resources to prepare, and are sometimes difficult to read.

What is meta-analysis?

Meta-analysis is a name that is given to a review article in which the results of several independent studies are combined statistically to produce a single estimate of the effects of a particular intervention or health care situation. The results of independent studies are lumped together to produce a number or a graph (usually with confidence intervals) that summarizes the effect of the intervention.[13] Other names given to meta-analysis include overview, quantitative overview, pooling, pooled analysis, integrative research review, research integration, research consolidation, data synthesis, quantitative synthesis, and combining studies. The main purpose of meta-analysis is to increase the precision of the conclusions of a review. This increased precision could:

- make comparisons of interventions more objective and accurate,
- help resolve controversies arising from studies with conflicting results,
- enable clinicians and patients to make better decisions,
- guide clinical research by generating new hypotheses,
- identify areas in which insufficient research has been performed or in which additional research may not be necessary.

Meta-analyses also have limitations. Some of these result from deficiencies in the individual RCTs they combine, which may have insufficient sample sizes, biased designs, be reported incompletely, or try to answer irrelevant questions. Meta-analyses, as the individual studies they include, are prone to bias of many types and from many sources.[19]

Are systematic reviews and meta-analysis the same thing?

Even though most people use the terms interchangeably, systematic reviews and meta-analyses are not synonyms.

How can a systematic review not be a meta-analysis?

A systematic review may incorporate state-of-the-art strategies to minimize bias and to maximize precision, but at the end, the reviewer may decide that the results of the individual studies included should not be combined. Data combination may be inappropriate for many reasons. For example, the studies may be too different in terms of their eligibility criteria, interventions, outcomes time points, the amount of data available, or methodological quality. Although necessarily subjective, assessing how much heterogeneity exists among studies included and whether they should be combined is one of the crucial steps in a systematic review. If, after evaluating the characteristics of the included studies, the reviewer decides that they can be combined, the systematic review includes meta-analysis and could also be called a *systematic quantitative review*. If a decision is made against combining the studies, the review is still systematic and should perhaps be called a *systematic qualitative review*. These two concepts are important for two reasons: first, because they define the distinction between meta-analyses that do and do not result from a systematic and scientific review process; and second, because they highlight the fact that not all systematic processes to review a body of scientific evidence should lead to the statistical combination of data across studies.

Is it possible to use meta-analysis in a review that is not systematic?

The minimum requirement to produce a meta-analysis is the availability of data from two or more studies, whether or not they were identified through a systematic search of the literature.

In response to repeated studies showing that most meta-analyses do not result from a systematic effort to synthesize the literature, many efforts have been made to improve their methodological quality. Perhaps the most important effort is that of an initiative known as QUOROM (QUality Of RepOrting Meta-analyses), which is similar to the CONSORT model to improve the quality of randomized trials.[20] It is not clear yet whether this effort has had or will ever have an impact on the quality of reporting of meta-analyses.

Needless to say, inappropriate meta-analyses may result in more harm than good. Reviewers and readers should understand that a systematic *qualitative* review of the literature, in its own right, is a more effective way to summarize the evidence than an inappropriate or misleading meta-analysis.

How can we evaluate the quality of a review?

The assessment of the quality of reviews, whether narrative or systematic, has the same challenges as the assessment of the quality of individual trials (Chapter 4). There are several published instruments for assessing the quality of reviews, but only one has been extensively validated[21] and published elsewhere.[22] This instrument, with slightly modified instructions, is included at the end of this chapter (Figure 6.1). Modifications in the instructions were made during the course of several empirical methodological studies to maximize inter-rater agreement. Another version of the instrument, in this case with major modifications, is included as part of the Users' Guides to the Medical Literature.[23]

Instructions

The purpose of this index is to evaluate the scientific quality (i.e., adherence to scientific principles) of research overviews (review articles) published in the medical literature. It is not intended to measure literary quality, importance, relevance, originality, or other attributes of overviews.

The index is for assessing overviews of primary ("original") research on pragmatic questions regarding causation, diagnosis, prognosis, therapy, or prevention. A research overview is a survey of research. The same principles that apply to epidemiological surveys apply to over-views: a question must be clearly specified, a target population identified and accessed, appropriate information obtained from that population in an unbiased fashion, and conclusions derived, sometimes with the help of formal statistical analysis, as is done in "meta-analyses." The fundamental difference between overviews and epidemiological surveys is the unit of analysis, not the scientific issues that the questions in this index address.

Since most published overviews do not include a methods section it is difficult to answer some of the questions in the index. Base your answers, as much as possible, on information provided in the overview. If the methods that were used are reported incompletely relative to a specific item, score that item as "partially." Similarly, if there is no information provided regarding what was done relative to a particular question, score it as "can't tell," unless there is information in the overview to suggest either that the criterion was or was not met.

For Question 8, if no attempt has been made to combine findings, and no statement is made regarding the inappropriateness of combining findings, check "no." If a summary (general) estimate is given anywhere in the abstract, the discussion, or the summary section of the paper, and it is not reported how that estimate was derived, mark "no" even if there is a statement regarding the limitations of combining the findings of the studies reviewed. If in doubt mark "can't tell."

For an overview to be scored as "yes" on Question 9, data (not just citations) must be reported that support the main conclusions regarding the primary question(s) that the overview addresses.

The score for Question 10, the overall scientific quality, should be based on your answers to the first nine questions. The following guidelines can be used to assist with deriving a summary score: If the "can't tell" option is used one or more times on the preceding questions, a review is likely to have minor flaws at best and it is difficult to rule out major flaws (i.e., a score of 4 of lower). If the "no" option is used on question 2, 4, 6, or 8, the review is likely to have major flaws (i.e., a score of 3 or less, depending on the number and degree of the flaws).

Index of the scientific quality of research overviews

1. Were the search methods used to find evidence (orginal research) on the primary question(s) stated?

　　□ NO　　□ PARTIALLY　　□ YES

2. Was the search for evidence reasonably comprehensive?

　　□ NO　　□ CAN'T TELL　　□ YES

3. Were the criteria used for deciding which studies to include in the overview reported?

　　□ NO　　□ PARTIALLY　　□ YES

4. Was bias in the selection of studies avoided?

　　□ NO　　□ CAN'T TELL　　□ YES

5. Were the criteria used for assesing the validity of the included studies reported?

　　□ NO　　□ PARTIALLY　　□ YES

6. Was the validity of all the studies referred to in the text asscessed using appropriate criteria (either in selecting studies for inclusion or in analyzing the studies that are cited)?

　　□ NO　　□ CAN'T TELL　　□ YES

7. Were the methods used to combine the findings of the relevant studies (to reach a conclusion) reported?

　　□ NO　　□ PARTIALLY　　□ YES

8. Were the findings of the relevant studies combined appropriately relative to the primary question the overview addresses?

　　□ NO　　□ CAN'T TELL　　□ YES

9. Were the conclusions made by the author(s) supported by the data and/or analysis reported in the overview?

　　□ NO　　□ PARTIALLY　　□ YES

10. How would you rate the scientific quality of this overview?

EXTENSIVE FLAWS		MAJOR FLAWS		MINOR FLAWS		MINIMAL FLAWS
□	□	□	□	□	□	□
—1—	—2—	—3—	—4—	—5—	—6—	—7—

Figure 6.1 Oxman and Guyatt's Index of the Scientific Quality of Research Overviews (information on its validation appears in Ref. [16], but the tool appears in Ref. [17]. Reprinted with permission.)

Do reviews on the same topic always agree?

As the number of published systematic reviews increases, we will often find more than one systematic review addressing the same or a very similar therapeutic question. Despite the promise for systematic reviews to resolve conflicting results generated by primary studies, conflicts among reviews are now emerging. These conflicts produce difficulties for decision makers who rely on these reviews to help them make choices among alternative health interventions where experts and individual trials disagree. A few years ago, one of us (A.R.J) proposed a tool in the form of a decision algorithm which could help in the interpretation of discordant reviews (Figure 6.2).[24,25]

Can rigorous reviews eliminate the need for further trials?

This is one of the most controversial and complex issues in health care research today. The controversy goes through a continuum: at one end are those who insist that if a rigorous meta-analysis shows evidence of effectiveness or harm for an intervention, it would be unethical to conduct anpagother study; at the other are those who regard meta-analysis, particularly of small trials, as untrustworthy and advocate for rigorous mega-trials to determine the effectiveness or harm of health care interventions. This controversy has been fueled by the publication of several studies showing frequent discrepancies, not only between the results of meta-analyses of small trials and large RCTs, but also among meta-analyses and mega-trials.[26–30] Possible reasons for the discordance between meta-analyses and large trials include major differences in the protocols and research questions, publication bias, and the inclusion of patient populations with different levels of risk in small and large trials.[25,31]

What is the role of the Cochrane Collaboration in all this?

The Cochrane Collaboration is an international organization that aims to help people make informed decisions about health, by preparing, maintaining, and ensuring the accessibility of rigorous, systematic, and up-to-date reviews (and where possible, meta-analyses) of the benefits and risks of health care interventions (www. cochrane.org). It was founded at a meeting of about 80 people from

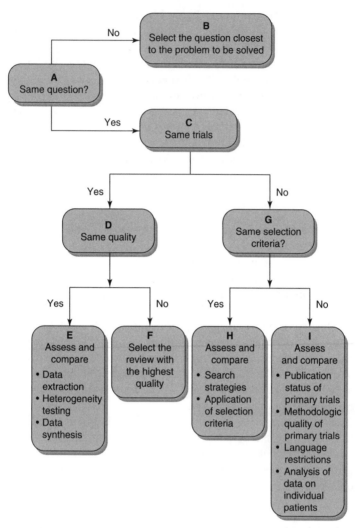

Figure 6.2   Algorithm to analyze discordant reviews (Reprinted from the *Journal of Clinical Epidemiology*, 45:885–892, Felson DT, ©1992, with permission from Elsevier.)

several countries who gathered in Oxford, England, in the fall of 1993.[32] The Collaboration is named after a physician-epidemiologist, Archie Cochrane, who more than 15 years ago, criticized the medical profession for not having organized 'a critical summary, by specialty or subspecialty, adapted periodically, of all relevant RCTs' to guide their clinical decisions.[33]

During more than a decade, the Cochrane Collaboration has had an unprecedented rate of growth. Nevertheless, this rapidly developing organization is also experiencing growing pains and facing important challenges.[34-36] Its long-term success will depend on whether it can keep maintaining and improving the quality of the reviews, ensuring that reviews are done of the most common therapies for important diseases, securing stable funding, making the format of the reviews more accessible for the average clinician, and motivating reviewers and funders to keep the reviews up to date.

The main product of the Cochrane Collaboration is The Cochrane Library.[37] As mentioned above, this is a regularly updated electronic library designed to give decision makers the evidence they need to make informed health care decisions, with special emphasis on data from RCTs. The Library was launched in April 1995 as The Cochrane Database of Systematic Reviews (CDSR). It was renamed to reflect the inclusion of additional important related databases, making it perhaps the most comprehensive source of information for all those interested in evidence-based health care (Chapter 7). It is issued quarterly and contains general information on the Cochrane Collaboration, a handbook on how to conduct systematic reviews, and the following databases:

- *The Cochrane Database of Systematic Reviews (CDSR)*: This is a rapidly growing collection of thousands of protocols and regularly updated systematic reviews of the effects of health care prepared by members of Collaborative Review Groups.
- *The Database of Abstracts of Reviews of Effects (DARE)*: This is a database of structured abstracts of thousands of systematic reviews from around the world, all of which have been completed outside of the Cochrane Collaboration. These reviews have been approved by reviewers at the National Health Service Centre for Reviews and Dissemination at the University of York, England. DARE also includes brief records of reviews that may be useful for background information, abstracts of reports of health technology agencies worldwide, and abstracts of reviews in the journals *ACP Journal Club* and *Evidence-Based Medicine* (Chapter 7).
- *The Cochrane Database of Methodology Reviews*: This is a database that contains a small group of systematic reviews of studies addressing common methodological challenges.
- *The Cochrane Central Register of Controlled Trials*: See above.

- *The Cochrane Methodology Register*: This is a database of hundreds of citations of articles on the science of research synthesis and on practical aspects of preparing systematic reviews.

In addition, The Cochrane Library provides easy access to thousands of health technology assessments and economic evaluations.

The Cochrane Library is available on CD-ROM and online, and should be regarded as an evolving product. More details on The Cochrane Library and on distributors can be found on the Internet.[38]

Should systematic reviews include only RCTs?

Even though most systematic reviews in health care focus on therapy and RCTs, the same approach could and should be used to summarize information produced in any other area of health care and by any other type of study design. It is still unclear, however, whether and how to use meta-analysis to complement systematic reviews in areas other than therapy (e.g. diagnostics, screening, natural history, health economics) and for studies other than RCTs.

Are there other organizations supporting the large-scale preparation of systematic reviews?

In 1997, the US Agency for Healthcare Research and Quality (formerly known as the Agency for Health Care Policy and Research) decided to fund a large number of Evidence-based Practice Centers (EPCs) in association with major organizations in the United States and Canada.[39] These centers perform systematic reviews with unprecedented levels of funding (several hundreds of thousands of dollars each) and breadth, in collaboration with prominent professional and community-based organizations in North America. The integration of reviews produced by the EPCs (which are not limited to RCTs) with existing Cochrane activities and the emphasis that is placed on keeping the reviews up to date, however, are limited.

Another large-scale effort worth mentioning is the Campbell Collaboration (C2).[40] It was created by 80 people who held an exploratory meeting at University College London in July 1999, and who went to establish it formally at a meeting at the University of Pennsylvania on February 24–25, 2000. The C2 is now a rapidly growing non-profit organization that aims to help people make well-informed decisions about the effects of interventions in the social, behavioral, and educational arenas. Although its focus is not health issues, the Campbell Collaboration has an enormous potential to complement its role model, the Cochrane Collaboration, particularly by bringing relevant evidence to policy makers.[41]

What is the difference between systematic reviews and clinical practice guidelines?

Clinical practice guidelines have been defined as 'systematically developed statements to assist practitioner and patient decisions about appropriate health care for specific clinical circumstances'.[42] These statements are usually presented as 'recommendations' for clinical practice and policy. Clinical practice guidelines represent a step beyond systematic reviews when their recommendations integrate research evidence from systematic reviews with the values and preferences of the developers of the guidelines and the context in which the guidelines will be applied. Systematic reviews *should not include recommendations* for practice or policy, but should be limited to providing a summary of the data available in the studies included and perhaps only *suggestions* for practice. Instead, they should be used as a component of clinical practice guidelines, providing the 'evidence base' from which recommendations are derived. Despite this, it is not surprising to find systematic reviews with very strong recommendations for clinical practice and policy.

Apart from an explicit process for deriving guidelines from the evidence, guidelines should consider all important management options. Guidelines on attention deficit/hyperactivity disorder, for example, should not simply look at the role of stimulants, given that there are other treatment options, including other pharmacological (e.g. antidepressants) and non-pharmacological therapies (e.g. dietary, behavioral or cognitive). Guidelines should also provide an explicit description of the strength of the evidence in support of a recommendation and the extent of the potential impact on clinical practice and policy if the recommendation is implemented.

Developing guidelines necessarily involves relatively small numbers of people with a limited range of views and skills. This is why it is important that the recommendations from such groups be evaluated and modulated by external review and comment from others who are interested in the problems addressed by the guidelines (e.g. a wide range of practitioners, managers, policy makers, and patients or their representatives) and tested in the field in which they are to be implemented.

Many practitioners distrust practice guidelines, and it is true that many guidelines should be distrusted. As with any other tool, including RCTs and systematic reviews, guidelines can be misused, especially when they are not based on a rigorous and objective analysis of current best evidence, or when they are used in settings very different from the one in which they were developed.[43,44] Just as with any source of evidence, guidelines can also be distorted by competing interests.[45] An increasing number of guidelines, however, provide practical recommendations based on sound evidence. Some, quite appropriately, even incorporate feedback from practitioners, and provide separate clinical and policy recommendations.[46] These sound evidence-based guidelines can help practitioners to improve the care they offer their patients.

The proliferation of guidelines has been such that ongoing efforts are being made to enable decision makers access as many as possible online, to avoid duplication of effort. One of such efforts, supported by the US Agency for Healthcare Research and Quality, is known as the Guideline Clearinghouse, a powerful resource that lists most guidelines produced in North America, enabling users to access them free of charge.[47]

What could be done when two or more interventions have been studied independently in different studies but never head-to-head?

One of the main challenges for efforts trying to make sense of a body of knowledge is the fact that most RCTs only include comparisons of up to a handful of possible interventions for a particular condition. As it was put bluntly recently, 'Seasoned scientific arguments, sponsors' agenda, marketing needs, ethics, regulatory dictates, perceived priorities, subjectivity on equipoise, exhibitionism in running a different trial, and arbitrary choices might lead to a complex mesh of diverse treatment comparisons. In this mesh, two treatments might never be compared head-to-head'.[48] In these very frequent cases, even the most powerful systematic reviews, meta-analyses or guidelines are left wanting. How to make sense of a complex and often patchy landscape of evidence, plagued by competing interests, opinions, prejudices, and preferences is what we will discuss in the next chapter.

Our musings

Although systematic reviews and meta-analyses are powerful tools to distill the evidence generated by individual trials, they are sometimes as misapplied as the trials themselves. As largely retrospective exercises, they could be easily manipulated by the reviewers. They cannot be expected to overcome the limitations of the trials they include ('garbage in, garbage out').

Like so many individual study reports, the bulk of systematic reviews in the biomedical literature conclude with the unsatisfying statement 'further research is needed'. It is also frustrating to see how the ability of systematic reviews and meta-analysis to identify gaps in knowledge has not translated into serious efforts by research funding agencies to fill them. A repeated call for systematic reviews to be a requirement as a preamble to any funding proposal for original research remains unheard.

Another unresolved problem relates to the need to keep reviews fresh, even for organizations such as the Cochrane Collaboration for which updating is one of its core values. There are a growing number of outdated reviews within The Cochrane Library.

The limitations of clinical practice guidelines, instruments that in theory could overcome the limitations of systematic reviews and meta-analyses, illustrate how our competing interests seem to know no boundaries.

References

1. Smith R. Medical journals are an extension of the marketing arm of pharmaceutical companies. *PLoS Medicine* 2005;2:e138. doi:10.1371/journal.pmed.0020138.
2. Mulrow CD. Rationale for systematic reviews. In *Systematic Reviews,* I Chalmers and DG Altman (Eds.). London: BMJ Publishing Group, 1995, pp. 1–8.
3. Smith R. The trouble with medical journals. *Journal of the Royal Society of Medicine* 2006;99:115–119.
4. Jadad AR, Rennie D. The randomized controlled trial gets a middle-aged checkup. *Journal of American Medical Association* 1998;279(4):319–320.
5. Jadad AR, Carroll D, Moore RA, McQuay HJ. Developing a database of published reports of randomised clinical trials in pain research. *Pain* 1996;66:239–246.
6. http://www3.interscience.wiley.com/cgi-bin/mrwhome/106568753/AccessCochraneLibrary.html (accessed December 22, 2006).
7. http://www.ncbi.nlm.nih.gov/entrez/query.fcgi?DB=pubmed (accessed December 22, 2006).

8. http://www.embase.com/search (accessed December 22, 2006).

9. Till JE, Phillips RA, Jadad AR. Finding Canadian cancer clinical trials on the Internet: an exploratory evaluation of online resources. *Canadian Medical Association Journal* 2003;168:1127–1129.

10. http://bmjupdates.mcmaster.ca/ (accessed December 22, 2006)

11. Greenhalgh T, Robert G, Macfarlane F, Bate P, Kyriakidou O, Peacock R. Storylines of research in diffusion of innovation: a meta-narrative approach to systematic review. *Social Science and Medicine* 2005;61: 417–430.

12. Mulrow CD. The medical review article: state of the science. *Annals of International Medicine* 1987;106:485–488.

13. McAlister FA, Clark HD, van Walraven C, Straus SE, Lawson FM, Moher D, Mulrow CD. The medical review article revisited: has the science improved? *Annals of Internal Medicine* 1999;131:947–951.

14. Schmidt LM, Gotzsche PC. Of mites and men: reference bias in narrative review articles: a systematic review. *Journal of Family Practice* 2005; 54:334–338.

15. Lau J, Antman EM, Jimenez-Silva J, Kupelnick B, Mosteller F, Chalmers TC. Cumulative meta-analysis of therapeutic trials for myocardial infarction. *New England Journal of Medicine* 1992;327:248–254.

16. Antman EM, Lau J, Kupelnick B, Mosteller F, Chalmers TC. A comparison of results of meta-analyses of randomized control trials and recommendations of clinical experts. *Journal of American Medical Association* 1992;268:240–248.

17. Cook DJ, Mulrow CD, Haynes RB. Systematic reviews: synthesis of best evidence for clinical decisions. *Annals of International Medicine* 1997;126: 376–380.

18. Akobeng AK. Understanding systematic reviews and meta-analysis. *Archives of Disease in Childhood* 2005;90:845–848.

19. Felson DT. Bias in meta-analytic research. *Journal of Clinical Epidemiology* 1992;45:885–892.

20. Moher D, Cook DJ, Eastwood S, Olkin I, Rennie D, Stroup DF, Improving the quality of reports of meta-analyses of randomized controlled trials the QUOROM statement. *Lancet* 1999;354:1896–1900.

21. Oxman Ad, Guyatt GH. Validation of an index of the quality of review articles. *Journal of Clinical Epidemiology* 1991;44:1271–1278.

22. Jadad AR, McQuay HJ. Meta-analysis to evaluate analgesic interventions: a systematic qualitative review of their methodology. *Journal of Clinical Epidemiology* 1996;49:235–243.

23. Guyatt G, Rennie D. User's Guide to the medical literature: essentials of evidence-based clinical practice. Chicago: American Medical Association Press 2002.

24. Jadad AR, Cook D, Browman GP. When arbitrators disagree: a guide to interpreting discordant systematic reviews of health care interventions. *Canadian Medical Association Journal* 1997;156:1411–1416.

25. Hopayian K. The need for caution in interpreting high quality systematic reviews. *British Medical Journal* 2001;323:681–684.

26. Bailar III JC The promise and problems of meta-analysis. *New England Journal of Medicine* 1997;337:559–560.

27. Cappelleri JC, Ioannidis JPA, Schmid CH, de Ferranti SD, Aubert M, Chalmers TC, Lau J. Large trials vs meta-analysis of smaller trials: How do their results compare? *Journal of American Medical Association* 1996;276:1332–1338.

28. LeLorier J, Gregoire, G, Benhaddad A, Lapierre J, Derderian F. Discrepancies between meta-analyses and subsequent large randomized, controlled trials. *New England Journal of Medicine* 1997;337: 536–542.

29. Villar J, Carroli G, Pelizan JM. Predictive ability of meta-analyses of randomised controlled trials. *Lancet* 1995;345:772–776.

30. Ioannidis JPA, Cappelleri JC, Lau J. Issues in comparisons between meta-analyses and large trials. *Journal of American Medical Association* 1998;279:1089–1093.

31. Furukawa T. Meta-analyses and megatrials: neither is the infallible, universal standard. *Evidence-Based Mental Health* 2004;7:34–35.

32. Sackett DL. The Cochrane Collaboration. *ACP Journal Club* 1994;May/June:A-11.

33. Cochrane AL. 1931–1971: a critical review, with particular reference to the medical profession. London: Office of Health Economics, 1979.

34. Jadad AR, Haynes RB. The Cochrane Collaboration – Advances and challenges in improving evidence-based decision making. *Medical Decision Making* 1998;18:2–9.

35. Laupacis A. The Cochrane Collaboration – how is it progressing? *Statistics in Medicine* 2002;21:2815–2822.

36. Grimshaw J. So what has the Cochrane Collaboration ever done for us? A report card on the first 10 years. *Canadian Medical Association Journal* 2004;171:747–749.

37. http://www3.interscience.wiley.com/cgi-bin/mrwhome/106568753/HOME (accessed December 22, 2006).

38. http://www.cochrane.org (accessed December 22, 2006).

39. http://www.ahrq.gov/clinic/epc/ (accessed December 22, 2006).

40. http://www.campbellcollaboration.org/ (accessed December 22, 2006).

41. Davies P, Boruch R. The Campbell Collaboration. Does for public policy what cochrane does for health. *British Medical Journal* 2001;323: 294–295.

42. Field MJ, Lohr KN (Eds.). *Clinical Practice Guidelines: Directions for a New Program.* Institute of Medicine, Washington, DC: National Academy Press, 1990.

43. Cook D, Giacomini M. The trials and tribulations of clinical practice guidelines. *Journal of American Medical Association* 1999;281: 1950–1951.

44. Shaneyfelt TM, Mayo-Smith MF, Rothwangl J. Are guidelines following guidelines? The methodological quality of clinical practice guidelines in the peer-reviewed medical literature. *Journal of American Medical Association* 1999;281:1900–1905.

45. Choudhry NK, Stelfox HT, Detsky AS. Relationships between authors of clinical practice guidelines and the pharmaceutical industry. *Journal of American Medical Association* 2002;287:612–617.

46. Browman GP, Levine MN, Mohide EA, Hayward RSA, Pritchard KI, Gafni A, Laupacis A. The practice guidelines development cycle: a conceptual tool for practice guidelines development and implementation. *Journal of Clinical Oncology* 1995;13:502–512.

47. www.guideline.gov (accessed December 18, 2006).

48. Ioannidis JP. Indirect comparisons: the mesh and mess of clinical trials. *Lancet* 2006;368:1470–1472.

CHAPTER 7

From trials to decisions: the basis of evidence-based health care

Health care decisions are usually the result of the interaction between the information available to the decision makers, their values and preferences, and the circumstances or context in which the decisions are made.[1] Randomized controlled trials (RCTs), even when assembled into a systematic review, are just one of the many different types of information that can inform decisions. In this chapter, we will describe some of the different types of information that can influence the role of RCTs in decision making, and how different values, preferences, and circumstances can process, modulate, and integrate information into our decisions.

What types of information can be used to make health care decisions?

Decisions can be influenced by both formal research studies and by information obtained informally, without the use of formal research methodology. This informal, or anecdotal, information can consist of anything we have learned from experience, our own or that of others, clinical or personal, directly or indirectly. Important as research from formal studies may be, the bulk of what we know still comes from our informal learning and experience.[2]

The interaction between different types of information in health care decision making is as complex and poorly understood as that between information, values, preferences, and circumstances. The first step toward exploring this complex interaction is to be aware of the different types of information that can be used to make decisions.

What are the different types of research studies?

Research studies can be either quantitative or qualitative.

What is a quantitative study?

A quantitative study is one that presents its results using numbers. Quantitative studies include *experimental* studies, in which the investigators influence the way in which the interventions are administered. (RCTs, the subject of this book, are one of the most important types of experimental study.) Other experimental studies include controlled clinical trials in which participants are allocated to the study groups using methods other than randomization (Chapters 1 and 2).

Some *observational studies*, in which the investigators do not influence the course of the events, are also quantitative studies. These studies can be controlled or non-controlled, and, depending on how the data are gathered, they can be prospective, retrospective, or cross-sectional. The *controlled observational studies* can be classified further into those with *contemporaneous controls* (studies in which data from the different groups are obtained during the same period of time) and those with *historical controls* (data from one or more groups are gathered at different points in time). Other things being equal, observational controlled studies with historical controls tend to favor the new intervention more frequently than those with contemporaneous controls.[3]

Specific examples of observational controlled studies include *cohort studies* (usually prospective with contemporaneous or historical controls) and *case–control studies* (retrospective and usually with contemporaneous controls). Surveys and cross-sectional studies are usually non-controlled. A detailed description of the different types of observational quantitative studies can be found elsewhere.[4,5]

Because RCTs have been more extensively studied, we know much more about them than we do about other study designs. Currently, we have a tendency to assume that RCTs are always better than other study designs. Sometimes this is wrong. It might be incorrect to give more weight to a flawed RCT than to a rigorous cohort study. The best form of evidence for a health care decision is the one that is appropriate for the particular problem.[6] For example, if the problem is *'What is the best initial treatment for uncomplicated hypertension?'* we would look to a well-conducted RCT, or better still, a meta-analysis of several well-conducted RCTs. If the problem was *'What is the best treatment for this particular woman with chronic asthma (rather than for asthmatic patients on average)?'* we would want to use an n-of-1 trial.[7]

What is a qualitative study?

A qualitative study is a study that does not attempt to provide quantitative answers to a research question. Rather, its objective is to try to interpret events or things in their natural settings and to develop conceptual frameworks about social phenomena.[8] In qualitative studies:

- Emphasis is placed on the meanings, experiences, and views of all participants.
- Major data collection methods include interviews, participant observation, or examination of documents.
- Hypotheses are usually developed during or after the research, rather than a priori.
- Established and evolving scientific methodology are used, accepting that some aspects of qualitative research, particularly those relating to quality of insight and interpretation, will remain difficult to appraise and will rely largely on subjective judgment.[9]

Are there different types of qualitative studies?

Yes. Some examples include in-depth interviews, focus groups, ethnographic studies, and case studies. A detailed description of qualitative studies, and their strengths and limitations was presented in a series of articles published by the *British Medical Journal*.[10] Frequently, two or more types are used to address the same issue. This strategy, which is known as *triangulation*, is used to compare the results obtained from different data collection techniques and study designs, and judge their robustness or validity.[11]

Are quantitative and qualitative research approaches mutually exclusive?

Often, a research question in health care is approached using either a quantitative or a qualitative approach, as if the approaches were mutually exclusive. This can be explained, at least in part, by the lack of experience or familiarity of most researchers with both approaches. A more coherent and efficient strategy might be to combine quantitative and qualitative approaches to answer research questions.[12,13] This could be achieved in a variety of ways: by using a quantitative study to guide the design of a subsequent qualitative study or vice versa; by conducting quantitative and qualitative studies simultaneously to answer a particular question; and by introducing elements of the one approach into the other (e.g. a quantitative study that includes some qualitative components).

The key should be to match the right type of design to the right type of question, or to the right aspect of a single question.

What is the role of non-research information in decisions?

Information can be obtained not only from research studies, but also from outside of formal research activities. This informally obtained information can have a profound influence on health-related decisions. Anecdotes, for instance, can be used to convey ideas, influence behavior, and make causal inferences. The use of narrative for the first two of these (to convey ideas and to influence behavior) is well established; its use for establishing causal relationships is much more controversial.[2]

We have a large and longstanding body of experimental research to show that narrative information is an effective and efficient vehicle for conveying messages and modifying behavior.[14,15] A number of independent but related elements contributes to the impact of this kind of information. One of the most important factors is that stories have emotional interest. The impact of a story depends in large part on that emotional interest. Things that happen to us personally are more interesting than those that happen to others; those that happen to people we know, respect or care about are more persuasive than those that occur to strangers or people about whom we have neutral feelings. Another important factor is the vividness of the information. Face-to-face recommendations have been shown experimentally to be more influential than even informationally superior data presented impersonally.[16] Health care recommendations by a respected local peer are a more powerful force for change in clinical practice than evidence-based consensus guidelines published nationally.[17]

The role of informal observation as a source of information to guide health care decisions is much more controversial. As human beings, we tend to make causal inferences from anecdotal information using simple rules of thumb, also known as *heuristics*. These are important because they allow us to quickly define and interpret the data of physical and social life, and to reduce complex tasks to much simpler operations. These rules of thumb are essential for everyday life, and will often lead to correct and useful conclusions. Data, either observational or experimental, can, however, be misperceived and misinterpreted. To the extent that motivation influences behavior, inferences can be distorted by needs and wishes.

The rules of thumb can sometimes lead us to incorrect and potentially harmful conclusions.

We should acknowledge the role of anecdotal information in health care decisions. Ignoring its powerful influence is likely to hinder communication among decision makers, and to retard their uptake of research evidence. Narratives can be used as vehicles to deliver the results of formal research to people involved in decisions, regardless of their background. Anecdotal information should be considered a complement to, rather than a replacement for, formal research evidence.

How can information be integrated into decisions?

Information is an essential component of making any non-trivial decision. At the same time, we have to realize that information is not enough to let us make valid decisions. No matter how much information is available, or how valid and relevant it is, it must always be modulated by the values and preferences of the decision makers, and the circumstances in which the decisions are made. In many (perhaps all) cases, our own values (both as consumer or provider of health care), our knowledge of other individuals involved in a particular decision, the particular characteristics of the setting in which the decision is being made, and our own previous experiences, will be at least as important as the more generalized evidence from even the best formal research studies.

In some cases the research evidence will be so compelling that it will be very difficult for anyone to ignore it, or to justify decisions that depart from it. In most cases, however, it will be unclear how much our tacit knowledge, anecdotal information, values, and preferences (and those of others involved in the same decision) will or should modulate the research evidence available. We, whether as clinicians, patients, public, or others who have to make health care decisions, have to walk the same fine line. It is the need to walk this line in safe and responsible ways that motivates those who responsibly support what is today called evidence-based health care.

What is evidence-based health care?

In many circles, evidence from research has become the accepted scientific standard for health care decisions. Evidence-based guidelines, evidence-based books, evidence-based medications, products, procedures, publications, what have you are proliferating widely and wildly. The term first popularized, *evidence-based medicine*, focused primarily on physicians and medicine.[18] It has since expanded to *'evidence-based health care'*, which goes beyond medicine to refer to all aspects of health care, with the simple and succinct definition of 'using the best research about the safety and effectiveness of specific interventions to help guide clinical decision making'.[19] Other terms since proposed include *evidence-based decision making*, which refers to the process itself, independently of the particular area or even outside health care;[20] and *evidence-based practice*, used by the US Agency for Health Care Policy and Research to designate a series of centers in North America, which have been charged with producing evidence reports and technology assessments to support guideline development by other groups.[21] More discipline specific terms have been emerging, including *evidence-based management*,[22] *evidence-based nursing*,[23] *evidence-based mental health*,[24] *evidence-based chaplaincy*,[25] and so on.[26]

What are the elements of evidence-based health care?

From what we have already described, any activity related to evidence-based health care should be:

- *Explicit*: clearly described and replicable.
- *Conscientious*: involving careful systematic steps to use research evidence as part of the decisions.
- *Judicious*, rather than blind adherence to research evidence.
- *Centered on the use of the current best available evidence from research*, not fixated on randomized trials or meta-analyses.
- *Aimed at informing and guiding decisions*, not at making decisions on the basis of information alone.

Although the term *'evidence based'* has been accepted jargon for some time, we (and we are certainly not alone) believe that it should be replaced with *'evidence-informed health care'* which more properly describes what we believe to be the optimal role for evidence in informed decision making.[27]

What steps should be followed during the practice of evidence-based health care?

The following steps of the process have been described in relation to evidence-based medicine and the care of individual patients, but could be applied easily to almost any other decisions in health care:[28]

- First, the decision maker must formulate answerable questions in relation to the decision being made (taking into account the elements discussed in Chapter 1).
- Once the question has been formulated, systematic efforts must be made to locate research evidence that could be used to answer the question.
- After identifying the research evidence, the decision maker should appraise its validity, relevance, and applicability.
- After appraising the evidence, the decision maker should be able to use it, integrating it with other types of information, his/her own values and preferences, and the circumstances in which the decision is being made.
- Once the research evidence is integrated with the other 'modulating factors' and used to guide a decision, the decision maker should make efforts to evaluate the outcomes of the decision and his/her own performance.

What are the potential advantages of an evidence-based approach to health care?

The understanding and application of the basic principles of evidence-based health care may help decision makers to:

- overcome the barriers that hinder adequate utilization of information as part of health care decisions;
- provide a common ground on which all decision makers could interact;
- enhance the appropriateness of practice and lead to better patient outcomes (as interventions of established efficacy become more widely used);
- spend resources more appropriately, as resources spent on interventions shown to be ineffective are transferred to more effective ones;
- identify knowledge gaps, leading to highly relevant new research efforts to fill these gaps.

What are the potential dangers of an evidence-based approach to health care?

The dangers associated with the practice of evidence-based health care usually result from misuse by decision makers. Both patients and clinicians could abuse evidence by paying attention only to research supporting their previously held views, while overriding contradicting evidence or other sources of information. Politicians, policy makers, and third party payers can also abuse evidence if they are more interested in financial stringency than improving health. For instance, if they ignore the fact (or do not understand) that a lack of evidence of effectiveness is not the same as evidence of a lack of effectiveness, these politicians and third party payers may decide to pay only for those treatments supported by strong evidence in order to save money or increase profits. Evidence can also be abused by sensation-seeking journalists, who are interested in 'breakthroughs' to make headlines, and therefore report only positive trials portraying them as the best available knowledge.

The practice of evidence-based health care can also become cult-like. Some decision makers may adhere to research evidence blindly, applying it in circumstances where it may not be appropriate, while ignoring its limitations, the role of other types of information, and the values and preferences of other decision makers. These dangers can be easily prevented by a proper understanding of the principles of evidence-based health care, which we have outlined above.

What barriers exist to the practice of evidence-based health care?

There are many inter-related barriers to the successful practice of evidence-based health care. Some of these are specific to individual decision makers, some to the nature of the available health care evidence, and some apply to the whole health care system.

What barriers apply to individuals?

Some of the more important barriers for individuals include:

- *Lack of awareness* of the potential benefits of evidence-based health care.
- *Lack of time*: Because of the existing reward systems and the increasing workloads of clinicians, the amount of time available to study and to keep up to date is likely to decrease rather than increase.
- *Lack of motivation*: Some decision makers may decide to rely more on informal methods for decision making.
- *Poor skills for question formulation*: Even if aware and motivated, some decision makers would fail to practice evidence-based health care simply because they do not know how to formulate answerable questions (Chapter 1).

Other barriers include inadequate literature searching skills and resources to access the literature; limited ability for critical appraisal;[29] and limited ability capacity to integrate research evidence with other types of information, values, preferences, and circumstances.

What barriers arise from the existing evidence?

Even when decision makers have optimal skills to practice evidence-based health care, they face many barriers emanating from the current state of research evidence. Some of the most prominent evidence-related barriers include:

- *Overabundance*: The amount of research evidence that is being produced worldwide makes it impossible for any individual to keep up to date, or even to find the valid and relevant material in the overwhelming body of literature.
- *Poor internal validity*: Many studies, including RCTs, lack the methodological rigor required to produce unbiased results (Chapters 3 and 4).
- *Limited relevance*: Few studies are designed with the day-to-day needs of clinicians and patients in mind. Many RCTs, for instance, have placebo controlled design, good to meet regulatory and academic needs, but inadequate to help clinicians and patients select treatments among the many options that have never been compared directly. Many studies also lack clinician and patient input during the selection of outcome measures. For example, most RCTs lack measurements of quality of life, patient preferences, or the resource implications of interventions, and few last long enough to produce meaningful answers.
- *Limited precision*: Most studies are too small to provide precise answers.

What barriers arise from the health care system?

The most important barriers imposed by almost every present day health care system include:

- *Lack of financial incentives*: Clinicians' performance tends to be judged by the number of patients they see and the resources they generate, rather than by how much they study or strive to make decisions based on the best available evidence.
- *Lack of training opportunities and effective training programs*: There are few opportunities for clinicians to gain the skills required to practice evidence-based health care. Even if more opportunities

for training were available, the effectiveness of the available teaching strategies has been questioned.[29,30]

How can we overcome the limitations to the practice of evidence-based health care?

Each of us must face our own blend of barriers and opportunities to the practice of evidence-based health care. As individuals, we must first identify those skills that we need to improve. We must also explore ways to make our own working environment more conducive to the practice of evidence-based health care.

Initiatives to improve the design, execution, and synthesis of research studies include the CONSORT and QUOROM initiatives (Chapters 4 and 5), and the Cochrane Collaboration (Chapter 6). There are a growing number of other important efforts to combine the best available evidence and the best available information technology:

- *Free access to MEDLINE on the Internet*: MEDLINE became available to clinical users in the 1980s and in 1997 it became free of charge on the Internet.[31] PubMed includes refined search strategies for optimizing searches for clinically useful studies.[32] Other vendors offer this for a fee.

- *Evidence-based publications*: This group of secondary or 'new breed' publications do the initial sorting of evidence using explicit methods to identify valid and clinically useful articles from a large number of journals, and then provide concise informative titles (Chapter 5), abstracts and commentaries that help readers discern whether the information applies to their own decisions. Surprisingly, these publications are typically thin and relatively infrequent in publication (e.g. bimonthly or quarterly), reflecting the fact that a very small proportion of the literature is really worth reading.

ACP Journal Club (ACPJC), the first of these 'evidence-based' publications, appeared in 1991. It was followed by *Evidence-Based Medicine (EBM)* in 1996, and *Evidence-Based Nursing* and *Evidence-Based Mental Health* in February 1998. Another example, *Bandolier*, is produced monthly by a group of leaders at Oxford which distill knowledge for easy use by decision makers worldwide.[33] Similar journals are likely to emerge in many other areas in health care. The main challenge will be to keep them full of valid and clinically useful content.

- *Specialized compendia of evidence for clinical practice:* Two superb examples are the Cochrane Library (Chapter 6) and BMJ's

Clinical Evidence. The latter provides an extensive list of other evidence-based resources available online.[34]

- *Evidence-based textbooks*: This even more recent development includes a group of textbooks that are kept up to date. These are still in their early stages, but are maintaining the basic principle (that declarations of what practitioners should do should be based on current best evidence), as they evolve. WebMD *Scientific American Medicine*[35] and *UpToDate*[36] demonstrate this, and are being joined by others.
- *Specialized web sites*: Clinicians now have a rapidly increasing number of online resources and organizations that could enable them to make evidence-based decision more accessible in practically all specialties and areas of interest.[37]

Our musings

Clinical care has been guided, for millennia, by expert authority, from Hippocrates and Galen to Pasteur and Lister. Randomized trials and evidence-based health care are relative newcomers to the field, far too recent to permit an objective picture of their place in clinical research, practice, or policy. Evidence-based medicine was hailed as a new paradigm when the term was first popularized,[38] less than two decades ago. It shook the accepted assumption that clinical experience and the study of basic mechanisms of disease are a sufficient ground for clinical practice, by shifting its foundation to information generated by randomized clinical trials and meta-analyses.

The initial proponents of evidence-based decision making claimed that clinicians whose practice is based on evidence from unbiased controlled trials would provide superior patient care. It demanded a whole new set of skills from practitioners, including an understanding of the rules of evidence, how to search, consult, and critically assess the research literature. It required time and resources not available in most busy clinical settings, and leaps of faith to extrapolate evidence from groups to decisions about care for individuals. Not surprisingly, the 'new paradigm' was challenged and initially rejected by those trained in the traditional manner.

Medical and societal attitudes toward evidence-based medicine changed at first slowly then almost unbelievably quickly. It was easy to recognize the value of randomized trials to show that some medications and procedures were more effective than others, or that many previously accepted practices were useless or even harmful. It was less easy to recognize how randomized trials could be subverted and used to generate useless or subtly misleading data. 'Evidence' could be used as a powerful form of rhetoric. Toward the end of the 20th century, 'evidence based' became the new mantra, the new slogan, the new authority.

The evidence-based paradigm has also started to be challenged philosophically.[39,40] The assumption that evidence-based health care is 'better' is reasonable and probably true, but it remains unproven. Ironically, there is little empirical evidence that evidence-based medicine works.[41]

Many other criticisms of evidence-based medicine are based on misperceptions, perhaps to a large extent engendered by the initial naïve enthusiasm of its early proponents. But concepts of evidence-based health care have matured and evolved.[42] Rather than a 'one size fits all' message, it now 'seeks to empower clinicians so that they can develop independent views regarding medical claims and controversies'.[43] Hopefully, in a not too distant future, patients and the public at large will be considered just as worthy of being empowered by evidence.[44]

Although we agree that evidence-based medicine has come a long way in the eyes of those who understand both its strengths and its limitations, we are concerned that in the public realm 'evidence based' has become the scientific face of health care, while 'Science' has become the new authority. We are further concerned that authorities, however well meaning, can be dangerous. We believe that the still present tendency to place RCTs at the top of the evidence hierarchy is fundamentally wrong. Indeed, we consider the very concept of a hierarchy of evidence to be misguided and superficial. There is no 'best evidence', except in reference to particular types of problem, in particular contexts.

While we recognize their value and importance, we are also concerned that overemphasis on randomized trials will divert scarce resources from more relevant research into the determinants of health and illness, and blind us to the vital roles of common sense, experience, and personal values in health care, as in all aspects of our lives.

Finally, a personal note: Both of us (ARJ and MWE) were, and are, strong advocates for RCTs, meta-analyses, and their incorporation into evidence-based decisions. We are proud of the research that we have done, and pleased (although a little embarrassed) by some of the accolades that our work has received. But we are also concerned that our initial zealous enthusiasm may have contributed to the unwarranted hegemony of randomized trial evidence. We hope that this book, and this chapter, will set the record straight.

References

1. Haynes RB, Sackett DL, Gray JRM, Cook DL, Guyatt GH. Transferring evidence from research into practice. 1. The role of clinical care research evidence in clinical decisions. *ACP Journal Club* 1996;125: A-14; *Evidence-Based Medicine* 1996;1:196–198.
2. Enkin M, Jadad AR. Using anecdotal information in evidence-based decision-making: heresy or necessity. *Annals of Oncology* 1998;9: 963–966.
3. Sacks H, Chalmers TC, Smith Jr H. Randomized versus historical controls for clinical trials. *American Journal of Medicine* 1982;72:233–240.
4. Altman DG. *Practical Statistics for Medical Research*, 2nd edition. London: Chapman & Hall, 2006.
5. Streiner DL, Norman GR. *PDQ Epidemiology*, 2nd edition. St. Louis: Mosby, 1997.
6. Sackett DL, Wennberg JE. Choosing the best research design for each question. *British Medical Journal* 1997;315:1636.
7. Patel A, Jaeschke R, Guyatt GH, Keller JL, Newhouse MT. Clinical usefulness of n-of-1 randomized controlled trials in patients with nonreversible chronic airflow limitation. *American Review of Respiratory Disease* 1991;144:962–964.
8. Fossey E, Harvey C, McDermott F, Davidson L. Understanding and evaluating qualitative research. *Australian and New Zealand Journal of Psychiatry* 2002;36:717–732.
9. Dixon-Woods M, Shaw RL, Agarwal S, Smith JA. The problem of appraising qualitative research. *Quality and Safety in Health Care* 2004;13(3):223–225.
10. Pope C, Mays N. Reaching the parts that other methods cannot reach: an introduction to qualitative methods in health and health services research. *British Medical Journal* 1995;311:42–45.
11. Payne S. Selecting an approach and design in qualitative research. *Palliative Medicine* 1997;11:249–252.
12. Sandelowski M. Combining qualitative and quantitative sampling, data collection, and analysis techniques in mixed-method studies. *Research in Nursing and Health* 2000;23:246–255.
13. Greenhalgh T. Integrating qualitative research into evidence-based practice. *Endocrinology and Metabolism Clinics of North America* 2002; 31:583–601.
14. Tversky A, Kahneman D. Judgment under uncertainty: heuristics and biases. *Science* 1974;185:1124–1131.

15. Greenhalgh T, Robert G, Macfarlane F, Bate P, Kyriakidou O, Peacock R. Storylines of research in diffusion of innovation: a meta-narrative approach to systematic review. *Social Science and Medicine* 2005;61: 417–430.

16. Redelmeier DA, Rozin P, Kahneman D. Understanding patients' decisions: cognitive and emotional perspectives. *Journal of American Medical Association* 1993;270:72–76.

17. Lomas J, Enkin M, Anderson GM, Hannah WJ, Vayda E, Singer J. Opinion leaders vs audit and feedback to implement practice guidelines. *Journal of American Medical Association* 1991;265:2202–2207.

18. Guyatt G. Evidence-based medicine. *ACP Journal Club (Annals of Internal Medicine)* 1991;14(Suppl 2):A-16.

19. Sakala C, Corry MP. What is evidence-based health care? *Journal of Midwifery and Women's Health* 2001;46(3):127–128.

20. Jadad AR, Haynes RB. The Cochrane Collaboration – advances and challenges in improving evidence-based decision making. *Medical Decision Making* 1998;18:2–9.

21. Atkins D, Kamerow D, Eisenberg GM. Evidence-based medicine at the Agency for Health Care Policy and Research. *ACP Journal Club* 1998;128:A-14–A-16.

22. Smith K. Evidence-based management in health care. In *Scientific Basis of Health Service*, M Peckham and R Smith (Eds.). London: BMJ Publishing Group, 1996, pp.92–98.

23. Ervin NE, Pierangeli LT. The concept of decisional control: building the base for evidence-based nursing practice. *Worldviews on Evidence-Based Nursing* 2005;2:16–24.

24. Bruce ML, Van Citters AD, Bartels SJ. Evidence-based mental health services for home and community. *Psychiatric Clinics of North America* 2005;28:1039–1060.

25. O'Connor TS. The search for truth: the case for evidence-based chaplaincy. *Journal of Health Care Chaplaincy* 2002;13:185–194.

26. Gray JAM. *Evidence-Based Healthcare: How to Make Health Policy and Management Decisions.* London: Churchill Livingstone, 1997.

27. Bowen S, Zwi AB. Pathways to 'evidence-informed' policy and practice: a framework for action. *PLoS Medicine/Public Library of Science* 2005;2:e166.

28. Sackett DL, Richardson WS, Rosenberg W, Haynes RB. *Evidence-Based Medicine: How to Practice and Teach EBM.* New York: Churchill Livingstone, 1997.

29. Norman GR, Shannon SI. Effectiveness of instruction in critical appraisal (evidence-based medicine) skills: a critical appraisal. *Canadian Medical Association Journal* 1998;158:177–181.

30. Sackett DL, Parkes J. Teaching critical appraisal: no quick fixes. *Canadian Medical Association Journal* 1998;158:203–204.

31. http://www.ncbi.nlm.nih.gov/entrez/query.fcgi?DB=pubmed (accessed December 22, 2006).
32. http://www.ncbi.nlm.nih.gov/entrez/query/static/clinical.shtml (accessed December 22, 2006).
33. http://www.jr2.ox.ac.uk/bandolier/ (accessed December 22, 2006).
34. http://www.clinicalevidence.com/ (accessed December 22, 2006).
35. http://www.hsls.pitt.edu/resources/documentation/sammedinfo.html (accessed December 22, 2006).
36. http://www.uptodate.com/ (accessed December 22, 2006).
37. http://www.clinicalevidence.com/ceweb/resources/useful_links.jsp (accessed December 22, 2006).
38. Evidence-Based Medicine Working Group. Evidence-based medicine: a new approach to teaching the practice of medicine. *Journal of American Medical Association* 1992;268:2420–2425.
39. Shahar E. A Popperian perspective of the term 'evidence-based medicine'. *Journal of Evaluation in Clinical Practice* 1997;3:109–116.
40. Tonelli MR. The philosophical limits of evidence-based medicine. *Academic Medicine* 1998;73:1234–1240.
41. Straus SE, McAlister FA. Evidence-based medicine: a commentary on common criticisms. *Canadian Medical Association Journal* 2000;163:837–841.
42. Sackett DL, Rosenberg WM, Gray JA, Haynes RB, Richardson WS. Evidence based medicine: what it is and what it isn't. *British Medical Journal* 1996;312:71–72.
43. Guyatt G, Cook D, Haynes RB. Evidence-based medicine has come a long way; the second decade will be as exciting as the first. *British Medical Journal* 2004;329:990–991.
44. Eysenbach G, Jadad AR. Evidence-based patient choice and consumer health informatics in the Internet age. *Journal of Medical Internet Research* 2001;3(2):e19.

CHAPTER 8

Ethics and clinical trials: are they compatible?

We take for granted today that a clinical research study should be ethical, and there seems to be general agreement on some basic ethical principles. Much of the apparent agreement disappears, however, when we try to put our ethics into practice. Ethics are neither a science nor an art. And they are much more than the decisions of a committee than can grant or withhold approval for a proposed research study. They are the way we live.

Ethical principles in research are the same as ethical principles in our ordinary day-to-day living. They are not learned by reference to principles, but by use, by analogies, by narrative, and by following role models.[1]

Randomized controlled trials (RCTs) are tools, in themselves value free. The extent to which they are ethical depends on how and why they are used. They can help to answer important health care questions that could not be otherwise answered, and when used for this purpose they are ethical, as long as the rights of all individuals concerned are safeguarded. They are not ethical when they are conducted primarily to meet regulatory requirements, for promotion of commercial or personal interests, or to satisfy the curiosity of researchers.

When can we ethically recommend participation in an RCT to our patients?

Before suggesting that someone participate in a trial, we have to first believe that the trial is worth doing. We should ask ourselves:
• Does it ask an important question?
• Will it help to provide the answer to that question?
• Would I participate in it myself?
• Would I invite someone I loved to participate in it?

If the answer to *any* of those questions is 'no', then the trial is not ethical. If it is not worth doing, it is not worth doing well.

Not all therapeutic decisions require evidence from an RCT. Sometimes the choice is not important, because the alternatives are too similar, or the problem does not really matter that much; it is not worth the cost and trouble of a formal comparison.

Sometimes we already know that one treatment is better than another; in this case, we should use it, not study it.

Often, however, even for important problems, we do not know which of possible or postulated treatments is best. Sometimes we do not even know if any treatment is better than letting nature take its course. We have no preferences. We are in a state of *equipoise*, of equal balance.

Equipoise is the ethical requirement that the researcher is genuinely uncertain as to the relative merits of the treatment alternatives in a clinical trial,[2] and provides good justification to proceed with a trial. We can, in this circumstance, ethically recommend to our patients that they should consider participation in the proposed RCT.

Why would someone participate in an RCT?

Benefiting others and advancing scientific knowledge are strong motivations for some people to participate in randomized trials. Others may be more driven by self-interest. Some may choose to participate in the hope of receiving better care or free services.[3] A number of demographic characteristics such as poverty, low educational levels, and old age are associated with willingness to participate. This raises concerns about the possibility of subtle coercion of such patients.[4]

A parallel question is why some people decide not to enter an RCT. A distrust of random allocation of treatment is a major factor. Many patients prefer either the doctor or themselves, rather than the play of chance, to make the treatment decision. Many patients express objections to being an experimental subject, a 'guinea pig'.[5]

Potential participants may have complex, sometimes competing reasons to decide to join or not join an RCT. Whatever their reasons, it is up to them to decide for themselves, without coercion.

Equipoise

Do we really need personal equipoise?

Clinicians or patients who believe, for whatever reason, that they *know* what is best cannot ethically participate in a trial. Patients come to clinicians for their professional advice as to the best treatment for their problem. Randomization would be ethical only if both the clinician and the patient are uncertain.

This presents a serious dilemma. Everyone concerned with a proposed RCT – researchers who plan the study, funders who may underwrite it, clinicians who may ask patients to enroll in it, policy makers who may use the results, and the patients themselves – almost always have their own preferences. If we insist on absolute *personal equipoise* to undertake or participate in a study – have no preferences whatsoever as to the result – few if any studies would be ethical,[5,6] few if any could be carried out, and many important questions would remain unanswered.

What about collective equipoise?

It is not the individual clinician, but the clinical community that establishes standards of practice. Allocation to experimental or control treatments in a study could be considered ethical if both are consistent with acceptable practice. *Collective equipoise* (also called *clinical equipoise*) means that clinicians, as a group, do not agree as to what is best among the available alternatives. Thus offering trial enrollment whenever there is professional disagreement within the clinical community is consistent with a clinician's commitment to the patient.

Nevertheless, if we grant total moral authority to the clinical community as a whole we devalue the responsibility of the individual clinician. Like individuals, the clinical community is fallible.[7] Reliance on collective equipoise may violate the trust between patient and clinician, one of medicine's core values.

An ethical clinician must take into account the received wisdom of her community, but always letting the patient know what she *really* believes is best for them. Sometimes this will be randomization. Sometimes it will not.[8]

Are there exceptions to the need for equipoise?

There are some situations when, even though we are confident that one intervention is better than another, an RCT can be ethically justified. Randomization is a fair way (probably the fairest) to allocate a treatment perceived (or confidently believed) to be effective to all who could benefit from it because of limited resources. This would allow a more rigorous confirmation that the intervention really is more effective, while ensuring that the short supply is fairly distributed.

RCTs can provide the evidence needed to challenge conventional practices, or to support innovative, but generally unaccepted, ideas. They can provide powerful rhetoric to convince 'hold-outs' within the clinical community. They can help establish the economic justification for interventions that remain controversial, despite evidence of effectiveness.

In situations like these, it is doubly essential that the potential participant completely understands the circumstances, be told the reasons why the trial has been proposed, and why they are being asked to participate.

Informed consent

Why do participants need informed consent for an RCT?

Every individual has a right to choose whether or not to participate in any randomized clinical trial, with access to as much of the available relevant information as they wish to have. They have the right to make that choice freely, with a full understanding of the issues, and without coercion. The ethical requirement for informed consent exists to protect those rights.

Why do investigators need informed consent for an RCT?

The primary purpose of informed consent is to protect the potential participant, not to protect the institution, the sponsor, the investigator, or the Institutional Review Board.[9] Nevertheless, documentation that the participant has been adequately informed is an important safeguard for the investigator, as they also have the right to conduct trials freely, without fear of legal consequences (when they do so on the basis of genuine equipoise and respect for the individual participant). For this reason written consent forms have become an institutional and legal requirement for research posing even a minimum degree of risk.

Although the written consent form also functions as a legal document, this should be a secondary, albeit important, purpose.

The primary purpose must be constantly kept in mind. Fundamental human rights come first, and are more binding than compliance with procedures and regulations.[10]

How does consent to an RCT differ from consent to clinical practice?

A randomized trial is not routine clinical care, even when all the interventions under study could be consonant with accepted practice. In clinical practice there is an unspoken implicit contract that all recommendations are made for the benefit of the individual patient.

In a randomized trial, however, the primary goal of the researcher is to test a scientific hypothesis.[11] Some decisions about care must be made on the basis of a protocol, rather than purely for the patient as an individual. Because of disparity in their power, this puts an even greater responsibility on the clinician investigator to adequately inform the patient.

Is informed consent always needed?

Plausible arguments have been made that requirements for informed consent should be waived in situations where all interventions offered in a trial are already available with no specific consent of the patient (e.g. advice, over-the-counter medications, educational materials). It has also been argued that informed consent could be waived when there is no additional risk from any of the alternatives, when genuine clinical equipoise exists among the treatments, where no reasonable person would have a preference for one treatment over another, or for additional use of biological samples obtained for clinical purposes.[12]

While such positions would certainly facilitate the carrying out of some useful RCTs without consent, we hold that they are still fundamentally unethical.

A greater problem may arise in emergency situations, with patients who are temporarily incompetent, such as from severe trauma, myocardial infarction, or stroke. Informed consent may be provided by a legal representative in such cases, but sometimes a representative is not immediately available. Physicians are empowered to provide emergency treatment in these circumstances, but the ethical and legal status of research for this population is not yet established.

Do participants understand the information they receive?

For consent to be informed, the prospective candidates for a trial must not only be made aware of the relevant information, but also must understand the issues involved in their participation.[13] Often this is not the case. Frequently, patients do not fully comprehend what they are being asked to consent to, or why, or how far their consent extends.[14] Although most participants feel that they have received the right amount of information, studies show that only half of them may feel that they understood it.[15,16] This could be due to linguistic, educational, psychological, or social factors. On occasion, however, this is the result of the complexity of the information available in the consent documents, driven by the need to provide legal protection to the host institution, to the researchers, or to the funders of the research.

From half to three-quarters of clinicians who enroll patients in randomized trials admit to believing that few of their patients understand the information given to them, even though they had given written consent.[17] Concepts like randomization, placebo, or double-blinding are particularly difficult to explain, and must not be glossed over. Asking questions to test patients' understanding of these concepts, and the reasons that we are using them, can help to avoid misunderstandings. Asking patients to fill out a brief questionnaire after they have read the consent form will both demonstrate their ability to read it and the extent to which the information is understood[18] (which can by no means be taken for granted).[19]

How can informed consent be improved?

Almost half of adults in high-income countries could be regarded as functionally illiterate in relation to health information.[20] In addition, most consent forms for participation in RCTs are written at or above the twelfth grade reading level, which is considerably higher than that of the majority of the population. Sometimes simple changes, such as the use of understandable language, can make an important difference. The text of informed consent forms can be readily written at a fourth grade level with no loss of content.[21] They can be written in simpler language and still retain all the essential information. This can result in significantly increased comprehension and lower levels of anxiety.

There is little research and little knowledge about the 'best' ways to share pertinent information about a trial with prospective participants, and perhaps there cannot, and should not, be rules or guidelines about this. One investigation that embedded an RCT in a qualitative study of recruitment strategies found that recruiters had difficulty discussing equipoise and giving equal value to alternative treatments as they presented them. They (we hope unknowingly) used terminology that was misinterpreted by participants. Changes in the order of presentation and clearer delineation of the treatment arms, along with discussion of the meaning of equipoise and of randomization significantly increased the recruitment rate.[22]

Relevant information can sometimes be shared more effectively by the use of modalities other than face-to-face discussion or printed information sheets. Multimedia information,[23] and particularly interactive applications, may be more useful and productive than traditional modalities.

How should we seek informed consent to participate in a trial?

It is not easy to ethically motivate patients to consent to participate in a clinical trial. Before we even start, we have to be sure that the study itself is ethical. This may demand some soul-searching, as well as considered approval by a research ethics board. The investigator must be thoroughly familiar with the aims of the trial and how it will be conducted. When possible, patient self-help groups should be involved in the research design.[24]

Discussion of clinical trial participation is sometimes seen as an intrusion into the clinician–patient relationship. It may undermine the patient's need, at a time of great vulnerability, to place their faith in a caring professional to navigate the route to an optimal treatment/outcome. This puts even greater onus on the clinician researcher to have, and use, sensitivity, compassion, and optimal communication skills during the recruitment process.

Who should be asked to participate in a trial?

It has been suggested that only patients who had previously expressed general willingness to be approached for research purposes should be considered for a specific RCT.[25] While novel and theoretically valid, if this became policy, it could have devastating effects on biomedical research and the advancement of knowledge. To presume that most patients inherently do not want to participate in research would deny those that do their right to participate.[26]

Can participants opt out of participating, rather than opting in?

The usual understanding of consent is that a patient must 'opt in' to participate in a clinical trial, even when the interventions to be tested may be widely available, and this seems inherently the most ethical approach. In rare situations, however, where the risk is very low (such as offering reading material), it might make more sense to assume that the patients would be willing to be in the trial unless they indicate otherwise, an 'opting-out' approach. In this modified procedure, a patient would be asked to sign a consent form to *not* be in the study.[27]

The opting-out approach results in a higher recruitment rate, and lower anxiety, and may produce a more representative sample of the target population.[28] The question remains as to whether and to what extent an 'opt-out' method of recruitment diminishes personal autonomy and could place people under increased risk of abuse by unscrupulous researchers. We believe that it should rarely, if ever, be used.

Is consent a singular event or a process?

Conventionally, consent is obtained only before a participant is enrolled in the trial. In acute situations, the patient or a surrogate may not adequately comprehend the situation or the nature of the interventions concerned, and yet timing of initiating the intervention is crucial. One promising approach to this, particularly when the intervention is ongoing and cannot be blinded, is to utilize a continuous consent process, in which further discussions with a senior clinician are used to ensure that the patient wishes to continue with the assigned intervention. This may improve the validity of the initial consent.[29] The crucial point is that the individual must really consent to what is being offered, and must be free to withdraw from the trial at any time.

How much information is required?

Investigators must share with patients all the information they need to decide whether or not they want to be in the trial. Research ethics scandals in the past have shown that sometimes important information was withheld. Now, however, the pendulum may have swung too far in the opposite direction; sometimes more information is presented than potential participants want, and can absorb or understand. The dictum 'the more information the better' does not always apply in real life. Brief information sheets can be better understood and remembered than longer ones. One size does not fit all.

This is particularly important for patients with life-threatening conditions, when choices between quantity and quality of life may be more affected by personal considerations than medical condition, and when the interventions are complex. Potential participants must understand their diagnosis, the nature of their condition, and the treatments options that are available, within or separate from the proposed trial.[30]

Are placebo controls ethical?

Whether or not a placebo control is justified depends on whether or not there is an intervention already available with proved or accepted value. When this is the case, the question should hardly arise; both the clinician and the patient will want to know whether a new treatment is more or less, effective or safe than a known effective intervention, not whether or not it is better than a placebo.

Nevertheless, even in these times of raised ethical consciousness, placebos are still commonly used in circumstances where their use is unethical. Many drug studies are conducted to meet regulatory standards that advocate or require use of placebo controls. This offers a clear benchmark to determine whether the new intervention is better than nothing, but tells us little about its benefit or risk compared with accepted alternatives.[31]

Practitioner as well as patient characteristics, and patient–practitioner interaction, may be major determinants of the placebo response. This is particularly true in the evaluation of complementary or alternative medicine.[32]

Proponents of active treatment controls point out that placebo controlled trials pay insufficient attention to the power of the placebo response. That people might receive a placebo, and the benefit associated with it is important and relevant information to help them decide whether or not to enter a trial. This information may not be innocuous, however, as it may reduce the complementary placebo effect of active treatment.[33]

Both defenders and foes of placebo controls agree that the interests of patients in clinical trials should not be compromised in the pursuit of new knowledge or profit, and that no one should forfeit the right to needed medical care because they are enrolled in a study. Every patient enrolled in a study should receive either the best option known to date or something new that is genuinely believed to have at least one advantage over the best available option (in terms of its efficacy, potential harms, associated cost, convenience, or attractiveness).[34]

What about vulnerable populations?

One reason that ethical codes are unequivocal about the investigator's primary obligation being to care for the human subjects of their research is the all too human temptation to subordinate the subject's welfare to the objectives of the study. Even with the most altruistic of motives, researchers may find themselves slipping over the line. Even informed consent is not protection enough, given the asymmetry in knowledge, authority, and emotional state between researchers and their subjects.[35]

Trials conducted in low-income countries with funding and protocols provided from wealthier countries have a variety of crucial ethical issues, including placebo or inadequate treatment controls, coerciveness, and exploitation.[36] Despite their scientific and clinical value, critics have argued that it is wrong to carry out trials in low-income countries that would not be considered ethical in the funders' wealthier home countries.[37] Others have complained that participants in these trials were coerced into participating because of their desperation. Whether or not this constitutes coercion is debatable; the potential participants are offered an opportunity that might improve their situation, not a threat.

The major criticism is that such trials exploit low-income countries and their citizens because the interventions in question, even if proven successful, may not be available to them. As a minimum requirement, those who participated in the trial should be guaranteed continued access to necessary treatment after the trial is concluded, and that the conditions for their participation would be equivalent to their counterparts in richer areas of the world.

A further concern is that trials may be conducted in low-income countries for the sole purpose of refining protocols (without need for registration), so that could be used subsequently in high-income countries to increase the chances of complying with the regulatory process.

Special situations

Are there special considerations for RCTs in surgical or other invasive procedures?

Randomized evaluation of surgical procedures is particularly difficult. Standardization is difficult because operators vary in their experience and ability. Differences in technique, and in perioperative and postoperative care may influence the outcome. The placebo effect of the interventions must also be considered.[38]

Blinding is difficult, often impossible. In the era before informed consent was a legal requirement, sham surgery was sometimes accepted and performed.[39] Ethical questions remain even when patients are informed of the possibility of sham invasive procedures. If there were some objective way of assessing the magnitude, as well as the probability, of harm caused by these surgical interventions, the determination that there is a favorable ratio of benefits to risks in the studies involving sham surgery might be credible. However, it is often difficult or impossible to make reliable assessments of benefits and risks in these cases.[40]

What about RCTs with pregnant women?

Ethical considerations for RCTs on pregnant women are essentially the same as those for all participants, with the additional consideration of the potential effects of intervention on the fetus as well as on the mother. This in no way justifies the exclusion of pregnant women from research studies,[41] but puts an additional responsibility on the investigator to be sure that the women fully understands the potential benefits and risks to the fetus as well as to herself.[42]

Are there special ethical concerns for community interventions?

Some interventions, such as information technology, or fluoridation of a water supply, must be administered to, and affect, entire groups of people rather than individuals within the group. In addition, interventions applied to only some individuals, such as behavioral interventions to stop smoking, may also affect others within the group who become aware of the interventions.

Special ethical considerations come into play when the unit of randomization is a community or cluster, rather than an individual.

In this situation, informed consent for participation cannot be obtained individually, because one person's choice may impinge on another's. Policy makers may put clusters of people into a trial without adequate consultation. The key ethical element is the welfare of the group as a whole, and careful procedural safeguards are required. Thoughtful consideration by an institutional review board is essential.[43,44]

Should health care professionals be paid for recruiting patients to trials?

Many RCTs fail to meet their recruitment targets, and hence do not have sufficient statistical power to test their hypotheses. One strategy to increase recruitment is to pay health care professionals to recruit subjects. Many pharmaceutical companies provide such inducement but this is not common in publicly funded research programs. There are important ethical issues concerning potential conflicts of interest, disclosure to patients, and the clinician–patient relationship. No controlled studies have been carried out on this topic.[45]

For anyone concerned (funders, institutions, ethics boards, researchers, clinicians, and even patients), there are likely to be major ethical problems with the trial when money makes a difference in recruitment.

Our musings

We have done a lot of musing about this chapter. Much of it is repetition of what seems obvious, and has been said by others before, ad nauseam. But despite this, the message does not seem to have been really heard.

The ethics of randomized trials reflect the values of those who propound them. They are valid only to the extent that the values that they reflect are shared. We believe that many of the values we express in this chapter are widely felt and espoused. We realize that some are not.

RCTs are powerful tools, almost wondrous in their power to separate the wheat from the chaff, to differentiate effective treatments from ineffective or harmful ones. So useful that it is often unethical to *not* do a randomized trial.

Tools are useful, though only when they are used properly, and used for the right job. They have to be used both well and wisely.

Most of the ethical problems associated with RCTs derive not from the tool, but from its misuse and abuse.

We are concerned that too many trials ignore the basic scientific principles that are so well known, and that we have emphasized in this book. A poorly conceived or poorly executed trial can result in misinformation, which is worse than no information.

We are concerned that sometimes potential participants in a trial are poorly informed about the purpose of a trial, or about the nature of the interventions to be compared. Sometimes information is glossed over, sometimes it is presented in overwhelming detail.

We think that information for informed consent should go far beyond the written word so beloved by lawyers and jurists. It should include, when appropriate, testimonials, videos, pictures, graphs, discussion, and decision boards. One size does not fit all. We have to think about the legal implications of these non-traditional approaches. Perhaps separating what is legal from what is ethical may help. In this way, a document could be signed by a patient after watching a video that really enables him/or her to understand what is being signed.

But our major ethical concern is not with the way individual trials are carried out, which will almost certainly improve as researchers become aware of how to correct errors in methodology or in how to better convey information. Rather, it is with integrity of the whole process that is meant to guarantee the ethical nature of a trial.

We know that often treatments that cry out to be tested are neglected. Not enough RCTs are carried out. But we also know that, because of commercial interests or misguided bureaucracy, sometimes too many unnecessary trials are performed.

It is hard to justify RCTs undertaken for trivial reasons, such as to comply with regulatory hurdles for a 'me too' drug. We are concerned that demonstrating a new drug or formulation to be better than placebo is at present enough for regulatory approval, without addressing the important question of how it compares with alternatives. If a head-to-head comparison with effective alternatives is not feasible because it would take an impossibly large sample size to show a significant difference, then the difference, if any, is insignificant. Why bother with a trial?

Competing interests come not only from industry (which invests vast amounts of funds in trials, hoping to get regulatory approval for their products to market as soon as possible), but also from the institutions or research groups that host trials (which are increasingly dependent on funds from those trials). These interests are so powerful that equipoise and informed consent are frequent casualties. For this reason we are concerned that institutional ethics review may themselves constitute a danger. We wonder why independent boards, who would not directly or indirectly benefit from the research, could not be the ones to decide on the appropriateness of a proposed trial. This could be even more valuable for multicenter trials, as coordinated research ethics boards could speed up the approval process, while avoiding duplication of the process in each participating institution.

We believe that research ethics boards should be transparent in their deliberations, and that there should be open disclosure of who funds the research and how the funds are disbursed, the amounts going to hospital, clinicians, and others. We would like to see a log of trials rejected by institutional ethics boards, with information about the overall budget, so we can see how representative funded trials are of the possible alternative hypotheses that could have been tested.

We think that there should be much stronger consumer representation on research ethics boards. As one public representative is a token, while two may succumb to a 'divide and conquer' situation we would like to see at least three consumer representatives on every research ethics committee. We believe that wherever possible consumer representatives who really represent those who will be affected by the trials (Arthritis Society for rheumatology trials, Cancer Society for oncology ones, and so on) should be involved in ethics boards.

Our musings could (and do) go on ad infinitum. Perhaps this is a good place to stop.

References

1. Cowley C. The dangers of medical ethics. *Journal of Medical Ethics* 2005;31:739–742.
2. Fried C. *Medical Experimentation; Personal Integrity and Social Policy*. Amsterdam: North Holland, 1974 (cited in Miller PB, Weijer C. Rehabilitating equipoise. *Kennedy Institute of Ethics Journal* 2003;13: 93–118).
3. Ellis PM. Attitudes towards participation in randomized clinical trials in oncology: a review of the literature. *Annals of Oncology* 2000;11: 939–945.

4. Fries JF, Krishnan E. Equipoise, design bias, and randomized controlled trials: the elusive ethics of new drug development. *Arthritis Research and Therapy* 2004;6(3):R250–R255.

5. Freedman B. Equipoise and the ethics of clinical research. *New England Journal of Medicine* 1987;317:141–145.

6. Weijer C, Shapiro SH, Glass KC. Clinical equipoise and not the uncertainty principle is the moral underpinning of the randomised controlled trial: for. *British Medical Journal* 2000;321:756–757.

7. Enkin M. Clinical equipoise and not the uncertainty principle is the moral underpinning of the randomised controlled trial: against. *British Medical Journal* 2000;321:757–758.

8. Lilford RJ, Jackson J. Equipoise and the ethics of randomization. *Journal of the Royal Society of Medicine* 1995;88:552–559.

9. Light IJ, The consent form: a time for reassessment. *Journal of Pediatrics* 1998;132:567–568.

10. Tognoni G, Geraci E. Approaches to informed consent. *Controlled Clinical Trials* 1997;18:621–627.

11. Donnellan P, Smyth J. Informed consent and randomised trials. *Journal of the Royal College of Surgeons of Edinburgh* 2001;46:100–102.

12. Truog RD, Morris AH. Is informed consent always necessary for randomized controlled trials? *New England Journal of Medicine* 1999; 340:804–807.

13. Flory J, Emanuel E. Interventions to improve research participants' understanding in informed consent for research: a systematic review. *Journal of American Medical Association* 2004;292:1593–1601.

14. Ashcroft RE, Chadwick DW, Clark SLR, Edwards RHT, Frith L, Hutton J. Implications of socio-cultural contests for the ethics of clinical trials. *Health Technology Assessment* 1997;1:1–67.

15. Ferguson PR. Patient's perceptions of information provided in clinical trials. *Journal of Medical Ethics* 2002;28:45–48.

16. Kodish E, Eder M, Noll RB, Ruccione K, Lange B, Angiolillo A, et al. Communication of randomization in childhood leukemia trials. *Journal of American Medical Association* 2004;291:470–475.

17. Edwards SJ, Lilford RJ, Hewison J. The ethics of randomised controlled trials from the perspectives of patients, the public, and health care professional. *British Medical Journal* 1998;317:1209–1212.

18. Melby T, Mendelson JE, Jones RT. Patients' understanding of consent form should be checked before participation in trial. *British Medical Journal* 1996;312:847.

19. Marcus EN. The silent epidemic – the health effects of illiteracy. *New England Journal of Medicine* 2006;355:339–341.

20 Paasche-Orlow MK, Taylor HA, Brancati FL. Readability standards for informed consent forms as compared with actual readability. *New England Journal of Medicine* 2003;348:721–726.

21 Coyne CA, Xu R, Raich P, Plomer K, Dignam M, Wenzel LB, et al. Randomized controlled trial of an easy-to-read informed consent statement for clinical trial participation: a study of the Eastern Cooperative Oncology Group. *Journal of Clinical Oncology* 2003;21:836–842.

22. Donovan J, Mills N, Smith M, Brindle L, Jacoby A, Peters T, et al. Improving design and conduct of randomised trials by embedding them in qualitative research: ProtecT (prostate testing for cancer and treatment) study. *British Medical Journal* 2002;325:766–769.

23. Mason V, McEwan A, Walker D, et al. The use of video information in obtaining consent for female sterilization: a randomised study. *British Journal of Obstetrics and Gynaecology* 2003;110:1062–1071.

24. Wager E, Tooley PJH, Emanuel MB, Wood SF. How to do it: get patients' consent to enter clinical trials. *British Medical Journal* 1995; 311:734–737.

25. Habiba M, Evans M. The inter-role confidentiality conflict in recruitment for clinical research. *Journal of Medicine and Philosophy* 2002;27:565–587.

26. Ilitis AS. Timing invitations to participate in clinical research: preliminary versus informed consent. *Journal of Medicine and Philosophy* 2005; 30:89–106.

27. Rogers CG, Tyson JE, Kennedy KA, Broyles S, Hickman J. Conventional consent with opting in versus simplified consent with opting out: an exploratory trial for studies that do not increase patient risk. *Journal of Pediatrics* 1998;132:606–611.

28. Junghans C, Feder G, Hemingway H, Timmis A, Jones M. Recruiting patients to medical research: double blind randomised trial of 'opt-in' versus 'opt-out' strategies. *British Medical Journal* 2005;331:940.

29. Allmark P, Mason S. Improving the quality of consent to randomized controlled trials by using continuous consent and clinician training in the consent process. *Journal of Medical Ethics* 2006;32:439–443.

30. Heaven B, Murtagh M, Rapley T, May C, Graham R, Kaner E, Thomson R. Patients or research subjects? A qualitative study of participation in a randomised controlled trial of a complex intervention. *Patient Education and Counseling* 2006;62:260–270.

31. Rothman KJ, Michels KB. The continuing unethical use of placebo controls. *New England Journal of Medicine* 1994;331:394–398.

32. Kaptchuk TJ. The placebo effect in alternative medicine: can the performance of a healing ritual have clinical significance? *Annals of Internal Medicine* 2002;136:817–825.

33. Skovlund E. Should we tell trial patients that they might receive a placebo? *Lancet* 1991;337:1041.

34. Baer N. Debate about placebos points to issue surrounded by many shades of grey. *Canadian Medical Association Journal* 1996;155: 1475–1476.

35. Angell M. The ethics of clinical research in the third world. *New England Journal of Medicine* 1997;337:847–849.
36. Brody BA. Ethical issues in clinical trials in developing countries. *Statistics in Medicine* 2002;21:2853–2858.
37. Lurie P, Wolfe SM. Unethical trials of interventions to reduce perinatal transmission of the human immunodeficiency virus in developing countries. *New England Journal of Medicine* 1997;337:853–856.
38. McLeod RS, Wright JG, Solomon MJ, Hu X, Walters BC, Lossing AI. Randomized controlled trials in surgery: issues and problems. *Surgery* 1996;119:483–486.
39. Cobb LA, Thomas GI, Dillard DH, Merendino KA, Bruce RA. An evaluation of internal-mammary-artery ligation by a double-blind technic. *New England Journal of Medicine* 1959;260:1115–1118.
40. Macklin E. The ethical problems with sham surgery in clinical research. *New England Journal of Medicine* 1999;341:992–996.
41. Enkin MW. The need for evidence-based obstetrics. *Evidence-Based Medicine* 1996;1:132–133.
42. McCullough LB, Coverdale JH, Chervenak FA. A comprehensive ethical framework for responsibly designing and conducting pharmacologic research that involves pharmacologic research that involves pregnant women. *American Journal of Obstetrics and Gynecology* 2005;193:901–907.
43. Edwards SJL, Braunholtz DA, Lilford RJ. Ethical issues in the design and conduct of cluster randomized controlled trials. *British Medical Journal* 1999;318:1407–1409.
44. Hutton JL. Are distinctive ethical principles required for cluster randomized controlled trials? *Statistics in Medicine* 2001;20:473–488.
45. Bryant J, Powell J. Payment to healthcare professionals for patient recruitment to trials: a systematic review. *British Medical Journal* 2005; 331:1377–1378.

CHAPTER 9
Reprise: more musings

Both of us have (for probably too many years) designed, conducted, published, systematically reviewed, synthesized, taught, critiqued, lived with, and suffered with, randomized controlled trials (RCTs). We have experienced the tremendous satisfaction that comes with successfully completing an RCT or a systematic review of trials. We know and appreciate the valuable contribution that RCTs have made to health care and to human health. We know the potential and the promise of well-planned, well-conducted, well-reported RCTs.

We accept that in practice RCTs have not always lived up to their ideal. They are human constructs, and as such are fallible. We recognize them as conceptually simple, powerful but vulnerable tools, which should be used with full realization of their limitations. We regret, but accept that there is no simple answer, no magical way to make RCTs always provide the unbiased evaluations that they, in theory, could. We fully realize that they cannot bring us everlasting truth, but believe that with care they can help us diminish everlasting error.

In our introduction to this edition we gave tribute to the pioneer of randomized clinical trials, Bradford Hill, and noted his disillusionment when he realized that RCTs can mislead as well as lead. Now, 40 years after him, we find ourselves feeling the same way, and echoing his thoughts. There has been real progress during these four decades. RCT methodology has improved, better measures have been designed to reduce bias and to make the evidence explicit, accessible, and useful. But the gaps between potential and practice that remain seem as great and as unbridgeable as ever.

This does not keep us from wishing, and hoping. We are cautiously optimistic, because we know that there are simple ways in which RCTs could, can, be improved. We have discussed many of these ways in previous chapters in this book. We believe our wishes are realistic and realizable. Perhaps those who share our goals and stand on our shoulders, and those who in turn will stand on their shoulders, will see our hopes or something better, fulfilled and come to pass.

Our main wish, from which all others stem, is that RCTs be taken off their pedestal, their exalted position at the top of an artificial evidence hierarchy; that all forms of evidence be appreciated for what they can offer. We wish that those who make decisions about health care think about RCTs as only one form of evidence, highly appropriate for some problems, less appropriate for others; and realize that no single form of research is best. We wish to see a diversity of research approaches, rather than a hierarchy.

We wish that the power of RCTs could be recognized and democratically controlled. We would like to see innovations tested and evaluated by independent bodies, made up of representatives of all groups who will be affected by the results of a trial: funders, investigators, clinicians, patients, regulators, and the public in general. We believe that trials should not be commenced until the protocol is agreed upon by consensus among those diverse interests.

New ideas and innovative interventions need to be both encouraged and evaluated by disinterested persons or groups. We believe that trials should be carried out by individuals who have no secondary gains or vested interests.

We wish incentives could be changed to encourage more relevant RCTs, ones that address important health problems rather than wasting resources on trivial issues, promote 'me-too' drugs or interventions, or are carried out simply to overcome archaic regulatory hurdles.

We wish for better RCTs, with more attention paid to known but often ignored sources of bias. This would include biases that influence a trial even before the first participant is enrolled, and those that continue even after publication of the results. We need trials that really answer the questions they set out to answer, and provide more valuable results, rather than the ubiquitous 'further research is needed'.

We look forward to better ways to present the results of trials to those who need the information, in a form that they can understand and use. We would like to see trials published soon after completion, regardless of the direction of their results, and made freely available in open access journals or online. We need systematic reviews of all RCTs, reviews that incorporate evidence from other sources as well, to provide guidance for policy and practice.

Above all, we need humility. The power of randomized trials, particularly as they feed into official health care guidelines, is enormous. They are a form of advice unlike ordinary advice; because of pressures to conform, there may be no option of refusal. The 'scientific evidence' has achieved a mythical status. It is excessively powerful rhetoric, a tool that so easily has become a weapon.

Evidence from RCTs is part of a complex information ecosystem, in which various sources interact, coexist, compete, and cooperate. To pretend that we can control this marvelously chaotic, uncontrollable, smorgasbord would be dangerous folly. But as freethinking, self determining human beings, we are major agents in this ecosystem. We can guide it towards a health promoting, rather than health diminishing evolution. To accept it, learn from it, and work with it is not only possible, but essential.

This is our reason for having written this book.

Alex and Murray

Index